The Theatre Student

CONCERT THEATRE

The Theatre Student

CONCERT THEATRE

Clayton E. Liggett

Illustrations by Martha Merrill

PUBLISHED BY

RICHARDS ROSEN PRESS, INC.

NEW YORK, N.Y. 10010

Standard Book Number: 8239–0194–7
Library of Congress Catalog Card Number: 72-104705
Dewey Decimal Classification: 792

Published in 1970 by Richards Rosen Press, Inc.
29 East 21st Street, New York City, N.Y. 10010

First Edition

Manufactured in the United States of America

TO MY FAMILY
AND
TO GOOD FRIENDS WHO WERE ONCE
MY STUDENTS AND TEACHERS

ABOUT THE AUTHOR

CLAYTON EUGENE LIGGETT has an exceptionally broad background as director of dramatic productions for high-school theatres, ranging from musical comedy and operetta, through contemporary drama, to Ibsen, Chekhov, and Shakespeare.

A native of Aberdeen, South Dakota, he received a B.A. degree from Buena Vista College, in Storm Lake, Iowa, and pursued postgraduate studies at the State University of Iowa, the University of Wyoming, the University of California at Berkeley, and San Diego State College. After periods as Speech and English Instructor and Drama Instructor in schools in Montezuma and Spencer, Iowa, he became Drama Instructor of the San Dieguito Union High School District, in Cardiff-by-the-Sea, California, where he is now Director of the Theatre, Instructor in Theatre and Stagecraft, and Chairman of the Department of Fine Arts. In these various posts he has directed some one hundred productions. He is also director of the San Dieguito High School Drama Chorōs, or verse choir.

A member of the American Educational Theatre Association, he served as panelist at the 1962 convention, on "Molière," and as chairman at the 1963 convention, on "Dance Theatre." He is also a member of the Secondary School Theatre Conference, the California Teachers Association, and the National Education Association.

Mr. Liggett makes his home in Encinitas, California, with his wife and their son and daughter.

ACKNOWLEDGMENTS

"Fred Basset" reprinted by permission of Publishers-Hall Syndicate and Associated Newspapers Ltd.

Dr. Faustus reprinted by permission of Caedmon Records, Inc.

The Menaechmi from *An Introduction to Drama* by Jay B. Hubbell and John O. Beaty. Copyright, 1927, by The Macmillan Company. Translated by Paul Nixon by permission of James Loeb.

Permission to reprint *Editha* granted by W. W. Howells, executor for the heirs of William Dean Howells.

"The Gift of the Magi" from *The Four Million* by O. Henry reprinted by permission of Doubleday & Company, Inc., publishers.

"Take My Hand" reprinted by permission of the Colorado Education Review.

"The Lord's Prayer" from *A Man Dies* reprinted by permission of St. James' Church, Bristol, England.

"Stopping by Woods on a Snowy Evening" from *Complete Poems of Robert Frost,* copyright, 1916, 1923 by Holt, Rinehart and Winston, Inc. Copyright, 1944, 1951 by Robert Frost. Reprinted by permission of Holt, Rinehart and Winston, Inc.

"Lucy Lake" from *Verses from 1929 On* by Ogden Nash, reprinted by permission of Little, Brown and Company. The poem originally appeared in *The New Yorker* magazine.

FOREWORD

Reading aloud by groups using all forms of literature has increased in popularity, especially in schools. No matter by what name it is designated, it is an exciting activity, involving many students and introducing them to a wide range of literary masterpieces.

Clayton Liggett, using the term *Concert Theatre,* knows what he wants and knows how to get it from his students. This book gives excellent details, interesting pictures, and workable instructions that are the result of Mr. Liggett's long and successful experience with this form of art. He writes what he knows and what he has done and what has worked to the delight of both performers and audiences.

Anne Simley*

---

* Miss Simley is Associate Professor Emeritus of Speech, Hamline University; Editor of Zeta Phi Eta *Cameo;* member of the Zeta Phi Eta National Council; Past National Secretary of Zeta Phi Eta; Past First Vice President of the National Collegiate Players; author of *Oral Interpretation Handbook, Stories to Tell or Read Aloud,* and *Folk Tales to Tell or Read Aloud;* and a recorder of taped books for the Library of Congress.

TO THE STUDENT

This text is for you, the student of the theatre; you may, however, let your teacher read it! Primarily, we will approach the subject so that you will be able to "learn and do" step by step while reading the book. We emphasize that you should pay particular attention to "do." Success in any art form comes from complete and enthusiastic participation in the art form. You will want the help of someone who understands the art. That is where your teacher comes into the picture. Also, you will wish the help of your peers who, by observing your participation in a group, will offer suggestions for improvement and will enhance your creativity with their imaginations.

Concert Theatre is entertainment in which at least one person reads from the printed page. Arrangement of the reader or readers is formal. The reader maintains his identity and therefore does not "become" his character physically. The locus is within the mind of the listener and not on stage with the reader.

The three basic types of Concert Theatre are (1) Readers' Theatre, in which standard-form play scripts are read; (2) Chamber Theatre, in which fiction, and at times nonfiction, is read; and (3) Choric Theatre, in which poetry and other forms of short, stimulating prose are read.

Concert Theatre—Readers' Theatre, Chamber Theatre, and Choric Theatre—is not a quick and easy road to performance. It is neither quicker nor easier than producing the material in staged-play form. Concert Theatre is an art form by and of itself. It is satisfying, exciting, and meaningful. Selfishly it is a means to self-improvement—great personal progress can be made while participating in any of the three types. Generously, Concert Theatre is a means of pleasing your audience—delighting them with a theatre form of which they are perhaps unaware.

Let us explain what Concert Theatre is *not*. First of all, it is not an inexpensive way to perform literature. Of course the cost of costumes and sets is practically nil, but to do Readers' Theatre only on the basis of saving money is an initial dire mistake. Some plays cannot be considered for Readers' Theatre. On the other hand, some material could not be feasibly staged and therefore is *best* for Readers' Theatre. Consider *Everyman*, Christopher Marlowe's *Dr. Faustus,* or Edith Wharton's *Ethan Frome.* Many of the German *Sturm und Drang* plays would be absolutely impossible for us to stage. Readers' Theatre and Chamber Theatre must not compete with staged plays—they are, and must be carefully so considered, an art form unto themselves.

Secondly, the Concert Theatre performances are not a short cut to public performance. None of the types is easy to produce well. Chamber Theatre is not merely reading the authors' material word for word. Choric Theatre is not a haphazard juxtaposition of unrelated material thrown out at random. Consider that without the visual aids of stage movement and business, costumes, and sets, much more demand is placed upon the reader and his ability to interpret meaningfully.

We certainly do not mean to discourage you before you begin—there are many advantages. Concert Theatre is a clean, sharp, sophisticated, and thoroughly satisfying way to entertain. A reader is himself. He is able to dress conventionally and, if he so desires, can mingle with his audiences during intermissions. Not burdened with props, costumes, regulated stage movement and makeup, he is accountable only to his vocal talent. He is free to identify with his audience and enjoy with them the charm of the material.

Recall with pleasure Paul Gregory's *Don Juan in Hell.* Remember Norman Corwin's *The World of Carl Sandburg* with Bette Davis. We did *The World of Carl Sandburg* both in Northwest Iowa and Southern California, and everyone was completely captivated—students, audiences, and performers. More and more state educational speech and drama associations are adding areas of Concert Theatre to their festivals and competitive meets. Professional speech and drama groups are including Readers' Theatre and Choric Theatre in their clinic and conference programs.

We look forward to the day when all forms of Concert Theatre are recognized as vital preparation in the secondary school. Concert Theatre offers so much opportunity for honest, gratifying learning and teaching. It is such a painless way to become familiar with quality material. Everyone feels a twinge of pride when he hears a familiar phrase from a classic piece of literature.

You are so fortunate! We assume that you and your teacher are excited about Concert Theatre and are "ready to go"! What fun is in store for you! Be greedy! Take all the enjoyment you can! Be generous! You'll give enjoyment too! Remember: "Do!"

—C.E.L.

Even Fred Basset feels pride when he utters a familiar phrase from a classic. (Permission granted by Publishers-Hall Syndicate Associated Newspaper Ltd.)

INTRODUCTION

The primary concern of any educational art form is the preparation of the student for a full and meaningful life in society. It is not to sell or exploit the talent of the student in public display. If the public performance can be done in harmony with the educational preparation, then additional merit for the art form is garnered. The educational art form encompasses many fields of which the majority of the public is unaware. We agree that music, theatre, dance, and art all come under this category. Many are unaware of the fact that the maneuvers and skills displayed on the athletic field are educational art forms. Neither are they aware that the sciences are art forms.

The artist, the musician, and the actor are heard at times to wail that they are not recognized. What does it mean to be recognized? They point with envy to the athlete, and they huddle together and nod knowingly at the government support of the scientist. And yet the creativity with which the three artists work would be suffocated in an environment of regimentation and control.

One prominent educator has said that to strengthen the country, everyone from kindergarten to college should study the creative arts on the grounds that they are more important than anything else in learning to understand life and society. Educate a new generation of poets and artists, some of whom could also handle the sciences, and this in itself would scare the Russians to death and take their minds off the nuclear threat.[1]

In the San Dieguito Union High School Department of Fine Arts, Division of Theatre, we educate on two levels. Both the participant and the spectator learn. The participant need not act nor interpret from the printed page to learn from the productions with which he works. The electrician, the set designer, the assistant, the costumer and staff, the makeup artists, the stage carpenter, the sound men, and the business manager have difficulty *not* learning techniques of directing and acting, production problems both contemporary and historical, and content of classics and contemporary literature. Through all of the many hours of preparation each student is learning to appreciate and evaluate this creative art. Your teachers are the first to realize that you may not have *immediate* appreciation of your study—years may pass, and often do.

The spectator learns much of what has been said. He at least is exposed to the various kinds of dramatic literature and is able to say immediately or at some later time, "Oh, yes, I remember having seen this. Now when I saw it before, it was done . . ." To accept or reject—but always with reason— is to appreciate.

A few years ago an "actress" came to us—confused and hurt. She had been told that she appeared in too many of the high-school productions—why were the "parts" not passed around more? She was ready to quit—"now and forever." We are glad that she did not: She now holds a responsible position with an outstanding television station and a degree in theatre. Others have

---

[1] Taylor, Dr. Harold, past president of Sarah Lawrence College. Keynote Address, American Educational Theatre Association Convention, 1962.

15

weathered much the same criticism: They too have succeeded at the Tyrone Guthrie Theatre in Minneapolis, on Broadway, and in network television. There are ever so many reasons an audience sees one individual in various roles during one season. Number one is that this individual has proven to be serious about the art, wants to *work,* and is being prepared for life in a society that he may well enjoy more because he is not content with the mediocre. While this individual is working, he is teaching just as surely as the director, and one day those who were holding minor roles will be teaching others.

Professional playwrights and directors know the worth of you high-school students and your work: "Broadway actors and actresses could learn much from the high-school thespian." [2] ". . . there were scenes which were never more meaningful upon the professional stage." [3] Care must be taken that opportunity *is* available for all those who seriously wish to take part. We usually offer four major productions, up to eight one-acts, and one or more types of Concert Theatre during each school year.

Concert Theatre—Readers' Theatre, Chamber Theatre, and Choric Theatre —is too often overlooked; it offers us areas in which to give experience to more students and to delight and instruct more spectators. Concert Theatre *is* theatre and belongs to you, the theatre student—a performing artist.

[2] Stong, Phil, author of *State Fair*. Personal letter, 1956.
[3] Hansen, Philip, creator of *Kings and Clowns* and director. Interview, 1964.

CONTENTS

ILLUSTRATIONS

The production photographs used in this book were taken by the following studios:

Plates I, II, III, IV, V, VI, X, and XI: Marvin Burk, Burk Studios, Spencer, Iowa.

Plates VII, XIII, XIV, XV, XVI, and XVII: Ron Dollimore, Dollimore Photography, Encinitas, California.

Plates XI, XII, and XIII: Rex Smith, Del Mar, California.

Chapter I

READERS' THEATRE

DEFINED

The definition of the various types of Concert Theatre is easily understood. Readers' Theatre is not an all-encompassing term to be used at random. The distinguishing feature is the material used—plays. Other forms of literature belong elsewhere. But not *all* plays should be done in Readers' Theatre. Information concerning kinds of material to be used will be taken up later. Readers' Theatre is performance by at least two people.

The part the audience plays is a point of definition of Readers' Theatre. It is important that the point of audience concentration (locus) be not onstage with you but rather within the minds of those listening. This may be difficult to understand. A staged play draws attention to itself, and the action (story-line) is happening right now. In *Arsenic and Old Lace*, when Mortimer lifts the lid of the window seat, he sees the corpse for the first time—*now!* Aunt Abby and Aunt Martha are doing their "good works" at this very instant. Teddy is concerned for the yellow-fever victims *while* the audience watches. In Readers' Theatre the performers are helping to recall, from the past, incidents within the story-line. The readers simply tell of the time, earlier, when Mortimer discovered the corpse. They relate that the action is occurring in some other place. The visual imagery is left to the mind of the listener (locus). Generally we offer no visual helps onstage.

However, there *are* exceptions, and we will cover them later in this chapter.

Readers' Theatre does not have to be read. We use the term Readers' Theatre because it is becoming a universal term with general recognition by most. No one will tell you that Readers' Theatre *must* be read. You *will* be expected to *appear* to be reading. We contend that if the play or cutting is properly rehearsed, memorization will be automatic—you will have gone over the material so much that at least partial memorization will be inevitable. Monologist Marty Barclay of Mason City, Iowa, who has performed throughout the eastern half of the United States, refuses to read a poem publicly until she has rehearsed it for twenty to sixty hours!

We believe that the script is your common link with your audience. Holding a script will give you added rapport with your listeners. Here is a group of theatre students "reading" so beautifully from the printed page—something tangible—something the listener could find and read. Hopefully your audience will also want to "do"—"get into the act." Perhaps you will have inspired them to organize one or more play-reading groups.

It is important that you rehearse with your scripts and use them effectively. A periodic glance at your script, even if you do not need it, is reassuring to your audience. Try Readers' Theatre completely memorized and do *not* use scripts—you will find it less effective.

All of the sections of this chapter help to form the definition of Readers' Theatre. As you read and reread various sections, you will be better able to sort out "that which is Caesar's." Please remember that the material we have included here is *descriptive,* not *prescriptive!*

ARRANGEMENT OF READERS

The arrangement of the readers is not completely apart from Chamber Theatre and Choric Theatre; you will want to work in a variety of arrangements. An arc used for Readers' Theatre may also be used in Chamber Theatre or Choric Theatre. The greater the variety, the greater the possibility of similar arrangements for Chamber Theatre and Choric Theatre. The reverse is true—one complements the other. The easiest arrangement is the simple arc; it is most often used. We suggest that you use this arrangement as a beginning. After you have a good start, you will want to use the other arrangements we shall explain and arrangements that you will create.

Sitting. The groups of readers sit in a simple arc on chairs (Fig. 1). When a narrator is used, he will sit apart from the basic arc. This will help your audience keep characters straight in more complex material. Two positions may be taken for reading within the simple arc. The cast may sit throughout the performance. A reader must be "with" the other readers when he is not reading. When he "enters" a scene and begins reading, he "comes alive" as the character. We prefer that those who are actually reading stand while they read. We have found that sitting reduces vocal energy. When the reader is no longer in the scene, he resumes his seat. When another reader enters the scene, he stands (Fig. 2).

Standing. We have witnessed Readers' Theatre during which all readers stood for the entire time. We cannot truthfully say we heard them! We were as weary when they had finished reading the play as we are sure they were! We *have* had one speaker stand and one sit on a stool—more for artistic grouping than any profound reason. The reading was Tennessee Williams' *Something Unspoken* (see Plate I). Because only two readers were involved, we did not want them to stand side by side, nor did we wish them to sit side by side. The play is not a tragedy, but neither is it a comedy, and it lends itself better to off-balance and angles than to symmetry. (See "Costumes, lights, and stage design" later.)

Stools. We are partial to the variations derived from stools rather than chairs. The stools may all be of one height or they may be of various heights. Stools are so nondescript that they will not "get in the way" of the audience—the audience will not be unduly aware of them. One can arrange himself more artistically, and if he wishes

Fig. 1. *Simple arc: basic arrangement.*

Fig. 2. *Reader stands.*

to rise, he can do so with more grace. Five 30-inch, six 24-inch, and four 18-inch stools will accommodate readers for most of the plays you will want to do.

Stools and lecterns. The professional Readers' Theatre groups often use stools with lecterns. The readers sit on stools of equal height behind lecterns. Their scripts rest on the lectern, and they lean forward slightly and place their hands on each side of the lectern as they read. When they are "offstage" they relax and place their hands comfortably in their laps or on their thighs (Fig. 3).

Miscellany. A variety of objects on which to sit may be used. We have used a combination of auxiliary steps, ladders, and stools in such presentations as *Dr. Faustus* (see Plate II). Obviously, with this kind of arrangement, parallel movement will be

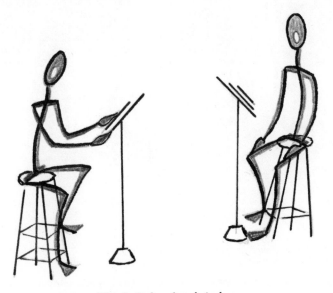

Fig. 3. *Relax, hands in lap.*

Plate I. *Tennessee Williams'* Something Unspoken, *Spencer, Iowa, Community School District. We chose finally to seat the readers on two levels. Note costumes, hands, place-ment of feet, hairlines.*

Plate II. *Marlowe's Doctor Faustus, Spencer, Iowa, Community School District. Every conceivable type of seating was used. Note levels and grouping.*

necessary. Another arrangement that is sometimes used is to have the readers sit on three sides of a table. We have never used a table for one basic reason: The table is a natural enemy of the rapport necessary between the readers and the audience—it comes between them. It is clumsy: If the table is the correct height for some, it is certainly much too high for others.

MOVEMENT

Movement means to move the entire body from one locale to another. Business means simply a justified gesture by the actor. Movement is used in Readers' Theatre; generally business is not. Basically there are three kinds of movement—each is identified in relationship of the reader to his audience: (1) parallel (sometimes referred to as lateral), (2) perpendicular (forward or backward), and (3) diagonal (at various angles).

Parallel. Parallel movement is generally limited to entering at the beginning of the performance and leaving at the conclusion. The readers move parallel to the audience. This is not to say that a reader never makes a parallel movement within the reading—he may. To deny all parallel movement will place unnecessary burdens upon the reader and the audience. *Menaechmi*, second century B.C. play by the Roman Plautus, basis for Shakespeare's *Comedy of Errors*, is a case in point. To maintain Menaechmus on stage right and Menaechmus-Sosicles, his twin, on stage left is to establish places of security and easy recognition. But to insist that their servants, Messenio and Peniculus, each stay with his own master or in his master's stage left or stage right place throughout would only serve to confuse the audience. This will be clearer as you read the script in Chapter II.

There is nothing wrong with parallel movement. In other texts on Readers' Theatre you may read that parallel movement is a "cardinal sin." If it enhances and makes more meaningful your presentation, employ it!

Perpendicular. Perpendicular movement is used without objection in most areas of Readers' Theatre. In the simple arc the reader stands as he reads (limited perpendicular movement) and may step forward (perpendicular movement). When he leaves the scene, he steps backward and/or sits (perpendicular). Note: If when moving backward, the reader is forced to take more than three steps, he should step backward two steps and then turn and return to his chair or stool—never turn immediately from a standing position—always take a step or two backward. If all the readers stand throughout, those in the scene must step forward as they read (perpendicular) to differentiate them from those not in the scene.

When using a stool the reader may never wish to stand, but to identify himself as being within the scene, he will turn full front (limited). If a lectern is used, he will lean forward (limited). If he *has* stood and moved forward to read, he will step backward (perpendicular) to resume sitting. If he does not stand, he will turn slightly from a full front to a closed quarter, or he will relax and take his hands from the lectern (limited). "Full front" is to face the audience directly. "Half closed" is turning away from the audience halfway—a profile. "Quarter closed" is halfway between "full front" and "half closed." "Full closed" is to turn your back on the audience, and "three-quarter closed" is halfway between "half closed" and "full closed." Each of these positions is important in its own way.

Diagonal. When miscellaneous objects upon which to sit are used (see "Arrangements" earlier), some of them will, of necessity, be placed upstage. This, then, will mean that the reader will move down (perpendicular), across (parallel), and/or at an angle (diagonal).

These movements are not to be considered dramatic as in conventionally staged plays. They are means to be seen, to be heard, and to make clearer the relationships of readers. They are functional rather than purely artistic.

COSTUMES, LIGHTS, AND STAGE DESIGN

Now we come to a part of Readers' Theatre that is a point of departure for authorities who, up to this point, have had some basis of agreement. We would guess that it is because Readers' Theatre is too often not placed in the hands of him to whom it rightfully belongs, the theatre student. Concert Theatre belongs to the theatre. We may assume that this is the reason it is called Readers' *Theatre*. Again—to ban absolutely the use of costumes, special lighting, and/or stage design because someone set down a rule is folly. If any one of these areas will enhance your performance and make it more meaningful, employ it! We *do* caution you that the audience locus is in their minds, and that care must be taken not to limit that imagination with visual aids that would be too definitive.

Costumes. Let us begin with suggestions for costuming that would be acceptable to most all "authorities."

Before we go further: Attention all boys: Always wear polished black shoes with black over-the-calf socks. Attention all girls: Maintain skirts at exactly the same length and never above the middle of the knee.

Speech and drama associations in various states specifically rule that there must be no suggestion of costuming when readers participate in competition. This seems honorable. So we have boys dressed in their "best," which may amount to one student wearing a suit, one wearing a sport coat, one a slack outfit, and one a slacks-and-sweater outfit because "I outgrew my suit and Mom says I can't get a new one now!" The girls seem better able to "go all-out" and they wear their best "party dresses"—plaids, dotted Swiss, satin, cotton, etc. *Each* reader looks handsome or lovely, but the *readers* are a hodgepodge of color and design shocking and upsetting rather than calming and preparing the audience to use their imaginations freely. The audience is more apt to interest itself in individuals rather than characters and the interpretation.

Unfortunately, we are becoming a society that demands that everything be done for it. Would you prefer that a novel be completely illustrated or have no illustrations so that you may imagine characters as *you* want them? Can you become interested in a radio story that leaves the appearance of charac-

ters and environment up to your imagination? It is to be hoped your answer will be "Please, I'd rather do it myself!" Dress your readers uniformly so they will blend as a unit and allow the audience to "dress" the characters with their imaginations.

We have fought the battle of costumes, and we prefer semimatching wearing apparel for everyone. The grade-school-program costume of black skirts and trousers and white shirts with black tie and white blouses leaves a great deal to be desired. Would you believe "The Midtown Waiters and Waitresses Guild"? A simple change of color solves this problem: navy blue complemented with pale blue. The result is unifying and pleasing.

Perhaps you will want to set apart the leads from the minor roles. Consider black for everyone except the leads. We managed *Faustus* nicely with black from the waist down—including tights. We double cast Faustus, and each boy wore a gray sweat shirt. Everyone else wore black sweat shirts and the girls "dressed up" the overall black with Peter Pan collars. Notice the use of headbands on the girls in the picture of the *Faustus* chorus. Make a rule for yourselves, girls: let your audience see your complete hairline. Hair styles should never allow the hair to be closer to the eyebrows than half an inch!

We are constantly on a tuxedo drive. When you acquire a quantity (so that every boy gets a "fit"), "costume" in tuxedos and white formals (see Plate III). If the formals become too extreme, here is another idea: *make* dinner gowns. We have a perennial sheet drive, too. Our girls had a great deal of fun designing their own dinner dresses from old sheets dyed gray. They were lovely, difficult as it may be to imagine. Each design had to be approved for overall style, propriety, and duplication. One girl sewed hers over and onto a strapless bathing suit, which served as an easy and excellent base. (At last report this girl owned her own modeling and design firm in Chicago. Perhaps the success of this design—among others—fostered her ultimate success; we would like to think so!) Single-strand pearls, single-pearl earrings, and white gloves fin-

Plate III. *Plautus'* The Menaechmi, *Spencer, Iowa, Community School District. A twelve-month tuxedo drive produces a stock of tuxedos to costume an attractive group of readers such as this one.*

ished each girl's ensemble. The black tuxedos and gray dinner gowns made a most pleasing picture and yet did not distract from the production material. The best part was the budget: *zero!* We stated earlier that readers may wish to mingle with their audience during intermission. The "sheet gowns" were nice enough to allow this. Caution: If free, dyed sheets are agreed upon, let no one buy new material because "I'll look nicer." It does *not* work—she will stick out like a sore thumb and ruin the overall effect.

How about uniformed clubs within your school? Pep-squad uniforms and letter sweaters become the school trademark for readers (not really a desecration!); pep club (ours have navy jumpers and white blouses, and the boys could wear navy trousers and white, short-sleeved, button-down shirts); choir robes. Trade with other schools if for some reason you do not want uniforms that are identified with specific clubs on your own campus. For all-male groups, black trousers with black combed-cotton turtlenecks, sleeveless, or T-shirts are striking against a black cyclorama (see Plate VI).

All kinds of combinations may be made of readily available uniforms; make use of your excellent imaginations! For a little added intrigue make outfits with colored fronts and black backs. Picture the possibilities against a black cyclorama when a few or all but a soloist turn their backs!

At times you will want to use true costuming—period costumes or costumes to specifically characterize. Generally this is reserved for Chamber Theatre, but use them for Readers' Theatre if they enhance, if their use is essential for clarity, or your presentation is in a manner of demonstration. For instance, costumes may be an integral part of your performance. A successful evening of eighteenth-century English comedy of manners playwrights may include three cuttings from one or more of these masters. The first selection done in period costume, the second in modern dress, and the third in a Readers' Theatre uniform.

Lights. It seems reasonable that lights are necessary! We speak here of special effects. Special lighting may be used to draw atten-

tion to a special reader or readers. Color may assist your audience to feel more completely the mood of the scene: e.g., blue or blue-green gel for Medea after she has killed her children. Blackouts in certain areas or of certain groups may be necessary to facilitate their actual exeunt or mental exeunt from the scene. Whatever lighting you use, whether it is purely functional or special, be certain that it is in good taste, pleasing, and does not draw undue attention to itself. Do not use special effects because they are clever in themselves. Back lighting (over the head of the reader) will help the reader see the script and will also put a nice reflected glow on his face. Fade the lights in and out to direct the audience's attention to various scenes in different areas of the stage. In the picture of *Doctor Faustus* you will see a sharply lit cobweb (Plate VIII). It was used for mood and did not appear "flashy." Ultraviolet light was played upon it, resulting in a glow that was in moderate contrast with the facial lighting seen through it.

Stage design. There is always stage design. As in all areas of this section, whatever you as the artist decide to do, whether it be costumes, lights, or sets, the result is a design. It may be very good, or it may be very bad—whichever the case, it *is* design. Fitting the parts to make a whole is creating an overall design; whether the reading takes place in a classroom, upon the stage, in a church, in the gym—whatever the environment, you will try to create a tasteful design.

We find that some visual aspects are necessary in the communities for which we have done Readers' Theatre. Such was the case with *Doctor Faustus.* The design was complete without the feeling of being staged. We have discussed the use of miscellaneous set pieces upon which to sit or stand. We described costume or uniform. The final step was a stage design to coordinate the parts, solo readers, chorus, seven deadly sins, and the stark appearance of two ladders, two auxiliary sets of stairs, and two stools. We actually tied them together with a web—skeletal in appearance, complementing the skeletal look of the set pieces. The center was established with two strings cross-

Plate IV. *Marlowe's* Doctor Faustus, *Spencer, Iowa, Community School District. Note use of headbands allowing for free and full use of facial expression.*

Plate V. Everyman, *Spencer, Iowa, Community School District. Sheet drives for inexpensive dinner gowns!*

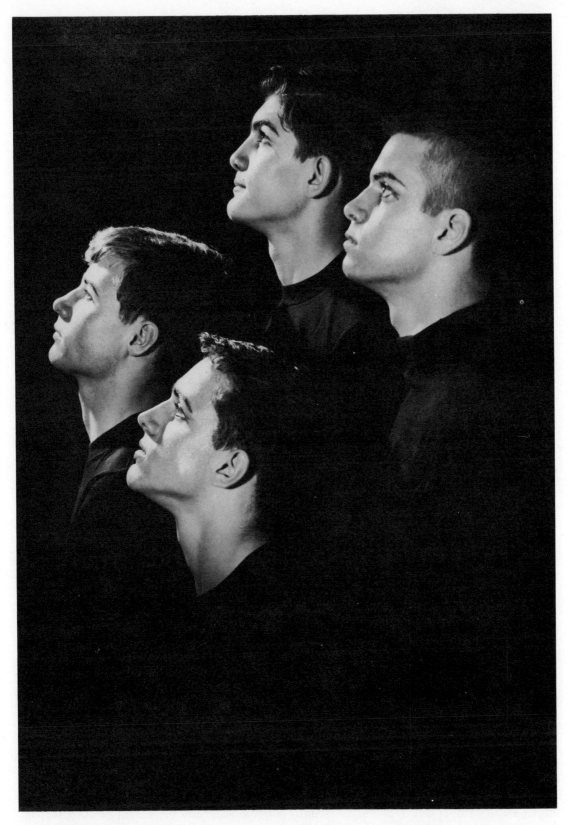

Plate VI. *Black combed cotton turtleneck T-shirts against a black cyclorama make for a dramatic effect.*

ing on stage right. Twelve other strings crossed at this point and were attached at their outer end to their first obstacle with pins, staples, or tacks. Starting at the center point, then, string was wound in a spiral as far out as possible (see Plate IV). Black light was played upon the center of the web and it faded out naturally as it reached

downstage left) to the center of the web. Moved very slowly, the spider is not unduly "clever" and becomes an integral part. The spider reached center as Faustus died.

The final bit of staging was the use of a puff of smoke from an electric powder box to cover Faustus as he died. We honestly report this and hasten to add that the ex-

Plate VII. *Readers' Theater, San Dieguito Union High School, Encinitas, Calfornia. Note suggestion of uniform costumes.*

the ends of the strands. The web was luminous. We carefully threaded a new ball of string through a small jar of luminous blue-white paint. We drew the whole ball of twine through the paint and stretched it back and forth across the gym to dry.

During the forty-five minutes of the reading, a cardboard spider was moved from the outer edge of the longest strand (above

plosion *was* too clever and too shocking and detracted from what had been a most successful evening in Readers' Theatre. Another time, Faustus would certainly not go up in a cloud of smoke!

In *Menaechmi* a drapery effect drawn by a white dove served only to add a point of interest and raise the height of what was an uninteresting and too horizontal design. Because the audience saw the simple arc of chairs and the drapery from the moment they entered the theatre, the design no longer demanded their attention once the reading began.

Borrow matching chairs from a local restaurant or upholstered armchairs from a fraternal organization. We used early American captain chairs for *Menaechmi*.

ners. The movement of the actors is so managed that they will also balance one another. This calms an audience so that they are in a spirit of gaiety (Fig. 4).

Asymmetry is achieved with balance but not necessarily equal numbers. We use asymmetry for a play or drama but not necessarily comedy or tragedy (Fig. 5). If a scene is amusing, the readers may move to

Plate VIII. *Marlowe's* Doctor Faustus, *Spencer, Iowa, Community School District. Mephistophilis, Chorus, Faustus. Note special lighting to direct attention.* (*See close-up of Chorus through cobweb, Plate IV.*)

It is important that psychological techniques used in acting and directing be employed in Readers' Theatre. You will want to refer to texts on these subjects for techniques too numerous to include here. The basic placement of readers and set pieces is within our realm.

For comedy, readers and set pieces are ideally placed in symmetry—stage balance. Notice the complete balance in pictures of sets for eighteenth-century comedies of man-

symmetry. If in Figure 4 the middle reader rises and moves behind one of the other readers, the result is off-balance used for a particularly serious moment in the play. Another move would be to have the reader on stage right move stage left and stand between the other two readers—the result is complete off-balance (Fig. 6).

Off-balance is most effective in tragedy and is interesting for the artistic picture in plays and dramas. A solo dramatic reading

Plate IX. The Menaechmi, *Readers' Theatre, Spencer Community Schools, Spencer, Iowa. Clayton E. Liggett, director.*

Fig. 4. *Symmetry: stage balance.*

is much more interesting when the reader sits off-center rather than center (Fig. 7).

KINDS OF MATERIAL

Not every play can be done in Readers' Theatre. We continue to maintain that a play is not a play until it is fully staged. An audience receives so much more from seeing a production than from reading a script. Theatre is an *active* art. However, Readers' Theatre is its own art and offers its audience an opportunity to supply individual imagination to material they may otherwise not have the opportunity to enjoy. When the material is based on dialogue, the play qualifies for Readers' Theatre. Farces that depend on stage business should not be attempted. If they are done without being fully analyzed beforehand, the group will begin adding bits of business, arguing that they *must* in order to make the audience understand. As more and more "essential" business is added, we end up with a staged production rather than Readers' Theatre, which is not *bad* but was not our original intent.

Do not be afraid to do such works as *Othello* merely because murders take place. The audience will accept the convention of Readers' Theatre that places upon them the

Fig. 5. *Asymmetry: unequal numbers.*

Fig. 6. *From symmetry to off-balance.*

responsibility of imagining major business. Greek plays, of course, are ideal because major physical conflict is only described, even in fully staged productions. The early English plays used in cycles are good because the lack of unity of place makes them difficult to stage. Since their purpose was to teach, there is much in the script alone for

Fig. 7. *Off-center solo reader.*

Readers' Theatre. We have mentioned the Roman play *Menaechmi*. Try *Abraham and Isaac, The Deluge,* or *The Second Shepherd's Play* from early English drama.

In addition to Marlowe's *Faustus, Volpone* by Ben Jonson offers such completely delineated characters that it is perfect material. Carlo Goldoni's *The Fan* depends too much on the fan itself as a property to be wisely used, but *Servant of Two Masters* is fun. *Servant* presents problems of mistaken identity such as in *Menaechmi* but they are not insurmountable. Because of the description instead of the actual battle, Pierre Corneille's *Le Cid* is a suggestion from seventeenth-century French classicism. Germany's *Miss Sara Sampson* by Gotthold Lessing and Russia's *The Inspector General* by Nikolai Gogol do well in Readers' Theatre. The list goes on and on, and the possibilities for production never end!

REHEARSAL TECHNIQUES AND INTERPRETATION

For any form of understanding, *three* is the magic word. Therefore, the first step in vitalizing your selection of a play for Readers' Theatre is to read the material three times. The first reading should be done as quickly as possible. This reading will "set" the story-line. The second reading is done with the audience in mind—their acceptance and appreciation of the basic material with what you know will be the limitations. Consider all possibilities for production in the third reading. Include possibilities of· previously discussed arrangement, movement, costumes, lighting, and stage design.

From the third reading on, each reader must begin to develop insight for his individual character. What is his background? His place in society? How does he think educationally, spiritually, politically? Know whether he is married (the script may not say—you decide). How many children has he—in what kind of home does he live? What kind of transportation does he use? What are his likes and dislikes with respect to food? What are his feelings toward other characters in the play? Are his feelings constant or are they reversed in other encounters—situations the audience does not see?

An excellent method of understanding a character is to "play through" or improvise his offstage experiences. For Thornton Wilder's *The Queens of France* we took each "queen" individually and "played through" her morning before the interview. We decided what her occupation was and put her in that situation. In one case she was a teacher asking her principal for time off to keep an appointment. In another case we added the "queen's" husband, and she prepared lunch for him and tried to make excuses for having to hurry and get out of the house to keep *her* appointment. Later we took all of the "queens" and played through a scene in which they all met with a mutual friend for a "coffee" later that afternoon. This mutual friend met one of the "queens" and greeted her with "What a beautiful dress! You look just like a queen!" The expression on the face of the "queen" when she heard that and suspected that her friend had found out her secret was marvelous! Do not try to do this play-through in the manner of Readers' Theatre; it will limit the possibilities of good development. We remember reading of a professional show that included a scene immediately following a wedding. To get the bride and groom in the correct frame of mind, a mock ceremony was performed in a dressing room with anyone who was free attending.

It is necessary from the very first rehearsal to read from the kind of script you will use in actual performance. The script must be on the exact size of paper, type, and folder that will be used for performance. The reader must get accustomed to the size of type; he must have the same amount of material and number of speeches on the same sides of the script; and his folder must be easy to use—he must feel secure that it will not fall apart! A uniform manner of holding the script must be decided upon and this manner used throughout all rehearsals. The scripts must be used as hand props; they cannot interfere with the reading or draw attention to themselves.

Other basics of rehearsal and presentation concern the visual aspects of the reader: sitting, moving, and audience contact. The

Fig. 8. *Posture* (*left, good; right, poor*).

Fig. 9. *Upstage foot on higher level.*

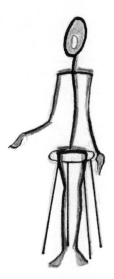

Fig. 10. *Feet on same plane: weakness.*

Fig. 12. *Upstage foot forward.*

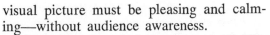

visual picture must be pleasing and calming—without audience awareness.

The back of a chair is *never* used! The reader should sit so that he is not tempted to slump and lean against the back. Neither should he sit so far to the edge that it is feared he will slip to the floor! Rehearse sitting posture from the beginning so that it will be second nature to sit up straight. It is so easy to slump and not be aware of how bad you look (Fig. 8).

Unless a reader is standing free, his feet should be on two levels. If he is standing on a ladder, the foot most clearly upstage should be raised to the next step. On a stool one foot is on the floor and the upstage foot is raised to the next rung (Fig. 9). On occasion, depending on the type of stool and the virility of the characterization or actor, this may be altered. Weakness is better illustrated with feet on the same plane (Fig. 10). Confidence is clearer with the feet on two planes (Fig. 9). Strength comes with more distance between the feet. Some boys will look best with one foot on the floor and the other foot two rungs up (Fig. 11). Or sitting on a chair or 18-inch stool, slide the foot most clearly upstage 3 or 4 inches ahead of the other foot (Fig. 12). Girls will also appear at ease with the toe

Fig. 11. *Upstage foot two levels up: strength.*

Fig. 13. *Upstage toe caught behind downstage heel.*

of the upstage foot caught behind the downstage heel (Fig. 13). At no time should the legs of any reader be crossed.

If at all possible rehearsals should be held in the environment in which the presentation will take place. When this is not feasible, try to arrange at least one run-through in the environment of the performance.

Interpretation. The playwright is a professional writer. He has spent long hours developing the story-line, theme, and characters within his work. It is our duty to interpret his work as carefully and intelligently as possible. Each and every word, thought, and idea must be given its due value. For those who are musically inclined, relate to note values—quarter, half, and whole notes. Strong words that should be emphasized are whole notes and must consistently receive full value—they must not be treated as half or quarter notes. On the other end of the spectrum, grace notes may be "thrown away" but with delicacy and forethought. *Think* understanding, *think* projection, *think* whole ideas. *Think* with the group and become a part of an ensemble. If you can maintain complete concentration, your battle is half won.

No actor should ever *act*—he must *re*act to his complete environment. It is far more difficult to *re*act than to *act*—it is far more satisfying to *re*act. In Readers' Theatre it is imperative to react because reacting is based on mental awareness and becomes in part physical. To act is to be aware physically and trust that that awareness becomes mental.

Listen to the other readers, *feel* a definite response. We use a reverse response technique constantly to promote awareness. For instance, reverse a negative response and make it positive. Your partner may be shocked—he listened. Do it again. The third time return to the negative and the response from your partner will be one of complete awareness. He will get that response as though it were for the first time.

In the third act of *Our Town* by Thornton Wilder, Emily asks the stage manager if she may go in to speak with her mother. Because Emily is dead and returning for the last time, her Mother does not respond. When Emily delivers the line after which her Mother *does* respond and sees her (playing a flashback), the actress playing Emily obviously knows this in advance. Without Emily's overhearing, have the Mother go right on working—ignoring Emily. Emily will stop, break, and question why the girl playing her Mother does not respond. Do it again. The third time the mother responds and Emily is relieved. It shows all over! This is the correct response—keep it!

To maintain the inner spirit of a character, we ask our students to create and maintain a psychological manner. The manner is not readily visible to the audience, but the whole characterization comes alive. Consider yourself a marionette; attach an invisible string to various parts of your body and let the manipulator draw the strings tight or let them fall; he will draw them straight upward or at angles. For a strong and secure Hamlet, the strings are taut and pulled upward. When he loses security and mourns for his father, all strings are loose— panic results with no true course of action. Mrs. Phelps in Sidney Howard's *The Silver Cord* is a proud woman whose psyche is self-righteousness. Her strings are attached to the crown of the head and perhaps slipped slightly forward—raising her chin upward— and pulled very tight for a strong, straight back; other strings are fastened to the shoulders and drawn up and backward. For weak characters draw the strings down—the crown-of-the-head string pulled down and to one side draws the head sideways and makes the character shallow and pathetic.

Other techniques of inner characterization are not only very helpful but also fun to develop. What animal does your character make you think of? Be that animal. What fruit? vegetable? color? texture? music? material?—use any abstraction. Carefully chosen music will help an actor feel the emotion of the character or scene. These techniques concern themselves with the inner person. We will not concern ourselves with techniques of physicalization for the actor.

We have mentioned the values of particular words—giving them full-strength value. This ability is made more difficult when we develop the tempo of our particular character. Our students are helped when each is assigned an inner tempo. If the tempo range in *Arsenic and Old Lace* is one to twenty and "one" is slow and old and "twenty" is quick, spirited, and young, Aunts Abby and Martha are tempo "three," Teddy is "twelve," and Mortimer is generally close to "twenty." Most all of the characters in the Lucille Ball situation comedies maintain tempos of "twenty-plus"! In the Andy Griffith Show, Andy is "twelve," Barney is "twenty," and Aunt Bea fluctuates from "four" to "eight."

You will succeed in emphasizing your more important lines by pauses and volume. Pause just before the key word; if the volume of the scene has been low, emphasize by increasing the volume; if it has been high, emphasize by a low key. Use the full range of pitch you have developed in your voice. Use it judiciously. Undercut your own speeches as well as the dialogue of your partner. That is, if the preceding speech has ended on a high note, begin your next line on a much lower note. The reverse is called topping: Top the low cue with a high note. The result is vocal variety.

Under most circumstances never let your partner finish the cue line. Cues are taken from the middle of the previous speech, not the final word or words.

"Can you remember the measurements of that front living-room wall?"

The cue is "measurements"—come alive.

"I get mixed up between the living room and the dining room, but I think the living-room wall is fifteen feet."

"Fifteen" is the cue.

"Fifteen! Oh no, it couldn't be."

In this situation the second speech ends with "fifteen feet," which is the pickup word for the third speech. In this case you cannot break into your cue speech before the cue word "fifteen."

Take the basics from what we have discussed here—arrangement, movement, use of costumes (uniforms), lights, design of the set, material, and rehearsal techniques and interpretation, and "do!" Let's discuss two ideally suited plays to work on for Readers' Theatre: *The Menaechmi* by Plautus and *The Tragical Historie of Doctor Faustus* by Christopher Marlowe.

Chapter II

SAMPLE SCRIPTS AND NOTES
FOR READERS' THEATRE

Two of our most satisfying evenings in Readers' Theatre were the evenings of *Doctor Faustus* by Marlowe and *The Menaechmi* by Plautus. Primarily we did them because they *need* to be done. They are important parts of theatrical history. *Faustus* is too little done both in high school and college because it presents problems that seem insurmountable. Readers' Theatre opens the way for more public presentations of this link between the medieval and the Shakespearean.

Why *The Menaechmi* is not done more often is indeed a puzzle. Its relationship to the *Comedy of Errors, Boys from Syracuse,* and now *A Funny Thing Happened on the Way to the Forum,* should place it high on the list of representative plays to produce.

Faustus was done with miscellaneous set pieces as we have discussed in Chapter I. We would repeat the cobweb effect. *Menaechmi* was done in the strictest sense of Readers' Theatre—that is, an arc of chairs, simple perpendicular movement, a minimum of lateral movement and interplay between characters, and no light changes.

(*Doctor Faustus* is under copyright by Caedmon Records—permission for production must be secured from them. Paul Nixon's translation of *Menaechmi* is no longer registered in the Library of Congress. Care must be taken when putting on a production for Readers' Theatre that permission be secured and that royalities be paid. Generally permission will be all that is needed. Many times Readers' Theatre productions are not required to pay the royalty governing completely staged productions.)

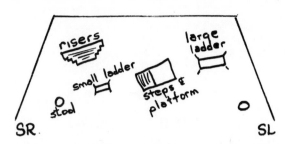

(Acting Edition)

THE TRAGICAL HISTORIE OF
THE LIFE AND DEATH OF
DOCTOR FAUSTUS

By Christopher Marlowe

(*Enter* CHORUS)

Chorus. Not marching now in fields of
    Thrasimene,
Where Mars did mate the Carthaginians;
Nor sporting in the dalliance of love,
In courts of kings where state is overturned;
Nor in the pomp of proud audacious deeds,
Intends our Muse to vaunt his heavenly
    verse:
Only this, gentlemen,—we must perform
The form of Faustus' fortunes, good or bad.
To patient judgments we appeal our plaud,
And speak for Faustus in his infancy.
Now is he born, his parents base of stock,
In Germany, within a town called Rhodes;
Of riper years to Wittenberg he went,
Whereas his kinsmen chiefly brought him
    up.
So soon he profits in divinity,
The fruitful plot of scholarism graced,
That shortly he was graced with doctor's
    name,
Excelling all whose sweet delight disputes
In heavenly matters of theology;
Till swollen with cunning, of a self-conceit,
His waxen wings did mount above his reach,
And, melting, Heavens conspired his over-
    throw;
For, falling to a devilish exercise,
And glutted (now) with learning's golden
    gifts,
He surfeits upon cursèd necromancy.
Nothing so sweet as magic is to him,
Which he prefers before his chiefest bliss.
And this the man that in his study sits!

(Divide chorus into light (L), medium (M),
and dark (D) voices. (A) indicates all
voices. We liked the effect of the chorus
coming on in a blackout.

Underline accented words and use perpendicular lines between words to indicate
pauses—one or two for short or long pauses,
which vary from the "ready-made" punctuation pauses. Arrow up (↑), high tone;
arrow across (→), medium tones; arrow
down (↓), low tone. Parentheses should
be preceded by a high tone and the paren-
thetical expression said in low tones. We
will not attempt to complete all markings
for you; that must be up to the particular
group and its director.)

BEGIN WITH ALL (A) VOICES

When a line of poetry ends with no punctuation, read with a slight lift to your voice—
a slight pause, then, accentuates the rhyme,
helps overcome a sing-song style, and at
the same time connects the two lines as one
thought.

(L)
(M)
(D)
(A)

(Faustus enters, sits on stool SL.)
(Fade lights on chorus as—)

SR.   SL

SCENE I

(Enter FAUSTUS in his study)

Faust. Settle thy studies, Faustus, and begin
To sound the depth of that thou wilt profess;
   having commenced, be a devine in show.
Is to dispute well logic's chiefest end?
Affords this art no greater miracle?
Then read no more, thou hast attained the
   end;
A greater subject fitteth Faustus' wit.
Be a physician, Faustus, heap up gold,
And be eternised for some wondrous cure.
"The end of physic is our body's health."
Why, Faustus, hast thou not attained that
   end?
Is not thy common talk sound Aphorisms?
Are not thy bills hung up as monuments,
Whereby whole cities have escaped the
   plague,
And thousand desperate maladies been
   eased?
Yet art thou still but Faustus and a man.
Wouldst thou make men to live eternally,
Or, being dead, raise them to life again?
Then this profession were to be esteemed.
Physic, farewell.—Where is Justinian?
A pretty case of paltry legacies!

His study fits a mercenary drudge,
Who aims at nothing but external trash;
Too servile and illiberal for me,
When all is done, divinity is best:
Jerome's Bible, Faustus, view it well.
Stipendium peccati mors est. Ha! *Stipen-*
   dium, etc.
"The reward of sin is death." That's hard.
"If we say that we have no sin we deceive
   ourselves, and there's no
truth in us." Why then, belike we must sin
   and so consequently die.
Ay, or must die an everlasting death.
What doctrine call you this, *Che sera sera,*
"What will be shall be?" Divinity, adieu!
These metaphysics of magicians

(—lights up SL on Faustus.)

(physician) *

(divinity)

(Don't omit the Latin.)

(K-sará-sará)

---

* Indicates special care and accent.

And necromantic books are heavenly;
Lines, circles, scenes, letters, and characters,
Ay, these are those that Faustus most desires.
O what a world of profit and delight,
Of power, of honour, of omnipotence
Is promised to the studious artisan!
All things that move between the quiet poles
Shall be at my command. Emperors and kings
Are but obeyed in their several provinces,
Nor can they raise the wind or rend the clouds;
But his dominion that exceeds in this
Stretcheth as far as doth the mind of man.
A sound magician is a mighty god:
Here, Faustus, try thy brains to gain a deity.

(*necromantic*)

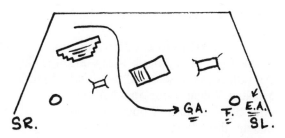

(Enter GOOD ANGEL *and* EVIL ANGEL*)*

(GA enters from USR and down to Faustus through center. EA enters SL and crosses to Faustus.)

G. Ang. O Faustus! lay that damnéd book aside,
And gaze not upon it lest it tempt thy soul,
And heap God's heavy wrath upon thy head.
Read, read the Scriptures: that is blasphemy.
E. Ang. Go forward, Faustus, in that famous art,
Wherein all Nature's treasure is contained:
Be thou on earth as Jove is in the sky,
Lord and commander of these elements.
(*Exeunt* ANGELS)

(Faustus looks up and out—no eye contact with the angels.)

Faust. How am I glutted with conceit of this!
Shall I make spirits fetch me what I please,
Resolve me of all ambiguities,
Perform what desperate enterprise I will?
I'll have them fly to India for gold,
Ransack the ocean for orient pearl,
And search all corners of the new-found world
For pleasant fruits and princely delicates;
I'll have them read me strange philosophy
And tell the secrets of all foreign kings;
I'll have them wall all Germany with brass,
And make swift Rhine circle fair Wittenberg;
O this cheers my soul!
For ere I sleep I'll try what I can do:
This night I'll conjure though I die therefore.

(Exit same way—GA lingers slightly.)

(Bolt 2′ x 4′ to top edge of a 10′ x 4′ piece of sheet metal and suspend offstage. Turn the bottom edge and attach two leather straps. Wave metal for thunder.)

(thunder)
(Lights dim slowly, brighten immediately.)

SCENE III (*A grove*)

(*Enter* FAUSTUS *to conjure*)

Faust. Now that the gloomy shadow of the earth
Longing to view Orion's drizzling look,
Leaps from th' antarctic world unto the sky,
And dims the welkin with her pitchy breath,
Faustus, begin thine incantations,
And try if devils will obey thy hest,
Seeing thou hast prayed and sacrificed to them.
Within this circle is Jehovah's name,
Forward and backward anagrammatised,
The breviated names of holy saints,
Figures of every adjunct to the Heavens,
And characters of signs and erring stars,
By which the spirits are enforced to rise:
Then fear not, Faustus, but be resolute,
And try the uttermost magic can perform.
Sin mihi Dei Archerontis propitii! Valeat numen triplex Jehovae! Ignei, aerii, aquatani spiritus, salvete! Orientis princeps Belzebub, inferni ardentis monarcha, et Demogorgon, propitiamus vos, ut appareat et surgat Mephistophilis. Quid tu moraris? Per Johovam, Gehennam, et consecratum aquam quam nunc spargo, signumque crucis quod nunc surgat nobis dicatus Mephistophilis!

(*Enter* MEPHISTOPHILIS *a Devil*)

I charge thee to return and change thy shape;
Thou art too ugly to attend on me.
Go, and return an old Franciscan friar;
That holy shape becomes a devil best.
I see there's virtue in my heavenly words;
Who would not be proficient in this art?
How pliant is this Mephistophilis,
Full of obedience and humility!
Such is the force of magic and my spells.
(Now,) Faustus, thou art conjuror laureate,
Thou canst command great Mephistophilis:

Mephistophilis is in during the change of lights. He rests script in his lap, his head is down, and his body is closed one quarter turn.

Eliminate the Latin—the idea of the Latin is maintained in shorter passages.

Meph. turns full open to audience, head up and script up.
(thunder)

Meph. closed one quarter, head down, script in lap.

(thunder)

(*Re-enter* MEPHISTOPHILIS *as a Franciscan friar*)

Meph. Now, Faustus, what would'st thou have me to do?

Faust. I charge thee wait upon me whilst I live,

To do whatever Faustus shall command,

Be it to make the moon drop from her sphere,

Or the ocean to overwhelm the world.

Meph. I am a servant to great Lucifer,

And may not follow thee without his leave;

No more than he commands must we perform.

Faust. Did he not charge thee to appear to me?

Meph. No, I came hither of mine own accord.

Faust. Did not my conjuring speeches raise thee? Speak:

Meph. That was the cause, but yet *per accidens;*

For when we hear one rack the name of God,

Abjure the Scriptures and his Savior Christ,

We fly in hope to get his glorious soul;

Nor will we come, unless he use such means

Whereby he is in danger to be damned:

Therefore the shortest cut for conjuring

Is stoutly to abjure the Trinity,

And pray devoutly to the prince of Hell.

Faust. So Faustus hath

Already done; and holds this principle,

There is no chief but only Belzebub,

To whom Faustus doth dedicate himself.

This word "damnation" terrifies not him,

For he confounds hell in Elysium;

But, leaving these vain trifles of men's souls,

Tell me what is that Lucifer thy lord?

Meph. Arch-regent and commander of all spirits.

Faust. Was not that Lucifer an angel once?

Meph. Yes, Faustus, and most dearly loved of God.

Faust. How comes it then that he is Prince of devils?

Meph. O, by aspiring pride and insolence;

For which God threw him from the face of Heaven.

Faust. And what are you that you live with Lucifer?

Meph. open full, head and script up.

Care must be taken that the readers do not hurry their lines merely to "get to the good parts." Marlowe created it all with much more thought than we are able to use. Give each word, phrase, and idea its full "musical value."

We sometimes call *"spit!"* meaning to enunciate. The word is short, sharp, and an easy direction so that the line reading is not interrupted.

Another word of direction is *"Lecture"* meaning: Say your words so that your "class" will understand better and could take notes!

Meph. Unhappy spirits that fell with Lucifer,
Conspired against our God with Lucifer,
And are for ever damned with Lucifer.
Faust. Where are you damned?
Meph. In hell.
Faust. How comes it then that thou art out
of hell?
Meph. Why this is hell, nor am I out of it.   (*is*)
Think'st thou that I who saw the face of
God,
And tasted the eternal joys of Heaven,
Am not tormented with ten thousand hells,
In being deprived of everlasting bliss?
O Faustus! leave these frivolous demands,
Which strike a terror to my fainting soul.
Faust. What, is great Mephistophilis so pas-
sionate
For being deprived of the joys of Heaven?
Learn thou of Faustus' manly fortitude,
And scorn those joys thou never shalt pos-
sess.
Go bear these tidings to great Lucifer: Meph. close three quarters.
Seeing Faustus hath incurred eternal death
By desperate thoughts against Jove's deity,   Dim SR spot on Meph.
Say he surrenders up to him his soul,
So he will spare him four and twenty years,
Letting him live in all voluptuousness;
Having thee ever to attend on me;
To give me whatsoever I shall ask,
To tell me whatsoever I demand,
To slay mine enemies, and aid my friends,
And always be obedient to my will.
Go and return to mighty Lucifer,
And meet me in my study at midnight,
And then resolve me of thy master's mind.
Meph. I will, Faustus.

(*Enter* GOOD ANGEL
and EVIL ANGEL)   GA in as before.
          EA in from SR behind Meph. and circling
G. Ang. Sweet Faustus, leave that execrable   up center and across to stand beside GA.
art.
Faust. Contrition, prayer, repentance! What
of them?
G. Ang. O, they are means to bring thee into
Heaven.
E. Ang. Rather illusions, fruits of lunacy,
That make men foolish that do trust them
most.
G. Ang. Sweet Faustus, think of Heaven,
and heavenly things.
E. Ang. No, Faustus, think of honour and
of wealth.

(*Exeunt* ANGELS)

Angels exeunt.

Faust. Of wealth! Why, the signiory of Emden shall be mine.

When Mephistophilis shall stand by me,

What God can hurt thee, Faustus? Thou art safe;

Cast no more doubts. Come, Mephistophilis,

And bring glad tidings from great Lucifer;—

Is't not midnight? Come, Mephistophilis;

(*Enter* MEPHISTOPHILIS)

(thunder)

Meph. open full.
SR spot up on Meph.

Now tell me, what says Lucifier thy lord?

Meph. That I shall wait on Faustus whilst he lives,

So he will buy my service with his soul.

Take care that there is no eye contact between characters. Rapport is achieved through meaningful delivery of lines.

Faust. Already Faustus hath hazarded that for thee.

Meph. But, Faustus, thou must bequeath it solemnly,

And write a deed of gift with thine own blood,

For that security craves great Lucifer.

If thou deny it, I will back to hell.

Faust. Stay, Mephistophilis; and tell me what good

Will my soul do thy lord.

Meph.   Enlarge his kingdom.

Faust. Is that the reason why he tempts us thus?

Meph. In company the miserable find solace.

Faust. Why, have you any pain that tortures others?

Meph. As great as have the human souls of men.

But tell me, Faustus, shall I have thy soul?

And I will be thy slave, and wait on thee.

And give thee more than thou hast wit to ask.

Faust. Ay, Mephistophilis, I give it thee.

Meph. Then Faustus, stab thine arm courageously.

And bind thy soul that at some certain day

Great Lucifer may claim it as his own;

And then be thou as great as Lucifer.

Faust. (*Stabbing his arm.*) Lo, Mephistophilis, for love of thee,

I cut mine arm, and with my proper blood

Assure my soul to be great Lucifer's,

Chief lord and regent of perpetual night!

View here the blood that trickles from mine arm.

Faustus does not actually stab arm. He reacts and delivers line as though he had memorized it!

And let it be propitious for my wish.
Meph. But, Faustus, thou must
Write it in manner of a deed of gift.
Faust. Ay, so I will. (*Writes*) But, Mephistophilis,

My blood congeals, and I can write no more.
Meph. I'll fetch thee fire to dissolve it straight.
Faust. What might the staying of my blood portend?
Is it unwilling I should write this bill?
Why streams it not that I may write afresh?
Faustus gives to thee his soul. Ah, there it stayed.
Why should'st thou not? Is not thy soul thine own?
Then write again, *Faustus gives to thee his soul.*

(*Re-enter* MEPHISTOPHILIS *with a chafer of coals*)

Meph. Here's fire. Come, Faustus, set it on.
Faust. So now the blood begins to clear again;
Now will I make an end immediately.
(*Writes*)
Meph. (*Aside.*) O what will not I do to obtain his soul.
Faust. Consummatum est: this bill is ended,
And Faustus hath bequeathed his soul to Lucifer—
But what is the inscription on mine arm?
Homo, fuge! Whither should I fly?
If unto God, he'll throw me down to hell.
My senses are deceived; here's nothing writ:—
I see it plain; here in this place is writ
Homo, fuge!
Meph. I'll fetch him somewhat to delight his mind.

(*Re-enter* MEPHISTOPHILIS *with Devils, giving crowns and rich apparel to* FAUSTUS, *and dance, and then depart*)

Faust. Speak, Mephistophilis, what means this show?
Meph. Nothing, Faustus, but to delight thy mind withal,
And to show thee what magic can perform.
Faust. But may I raise up spirits when I please?

Use script to read. Do not write. Memorize second sentence.

(faint thunder)

Meph. head down, script down.

No chafer of coals.
(faint thunder)
Meph. head and script up.

Simply extend hand forward, palm up. For any gesture such as this one, begin early and finish late—always slowly—*very* slowly!

(Hōmō-few′-gay)

Cut "somewhat" and add "devils."
Meph. head and book down as music begins.
(Flute and piccolo music ad lib.)

(Music played under lines.)
No "devils" are seen.
Meph. head up.

Both look out over center of audience and "watch" Devils.

Meph. Ay, Faustus, and do greater things than these.

Faust. Then there's enough for a thousand souls.

Here, Mephistophilis, receive this scroll,

A deed of gift of body and of soul:

But yet conditionally that thou perform

All articles prescribed between us both.

Meph. Faustus, I swear by hell and Lucifer

To effect all promises between us made.

Speak, Faustus, do you deliver this as your deed?

Faust. Ay, take it, and the Devil give thee good on't.

Meph. Now, Faustus, ask what thou wilt.

Faust. First will I question with thee about hell.

Tell me where is the place that men call hell?

Meph. Under the heavens.

Faust. Ay, but whereabout?

Meph. Within the bowels of these elements,

Where we are tortured and remain for ever;

Hell hath no limits, nor is circumscribed

In one self place; for where we are is hell,

And where hell is there we must ever be:

And, to conclude, when all the world dissolves,

And every creature shall be purified,

All places shall be hell that is not Heaven.

Faust. Come, I think hell's a fable.

Meph. Ay, think so still, till experience change thy mind.

Faust. Why, think'st thou then that Faustus shall be damned?

Meph. Ay, of necessity, for here's the scroll

Wherein thou hast given thy soul to Lucifer.

Faust. Ay, and body too; but what of that?

Think'st thou that Faustus is so fond to imagine

That, after this life, there is any pain?

Tush; these are trifles, and mere old wives' tales.

Meph. But, Faustus, I am an instance to prove the contrary,

For I am damned, and am now in hell.

Faust. How! now in hell!

Nay, an this be hell, I'll willingly be damned here;

What? walking, disputing, etc.?

But, leaving this off, let me have a wife,

The fairest maid in Germany;

(Music fades.)

Again, simple gestures forward to "give" and "receive" scroll.

Memorize!

Whenever the diction seems to be faulty we rewrite the words in the text: "What of that" is rewritten "wha tuv that." The result is amazing!

For I am wanton and lascivious,
And cannot live without a wife.
Meph. How—a wife?
I prithee, Faustus, talk not of a wife.
Faust. Nay, sweet Mephistophilis, fetch me
   one, for I will have one.
Meph. Well—thou wilt have one. Sit there
   till I come:
I'll fetch thee a wife in the Devil's name.

        (*Exit*)

(*Re-enter* MEPHISTOPHILIS *with a Devil
      dressed as a woman*)

(Flute music up.)
Do not add devil character.

Meph. Tell (me) Faustus, how dost thou
   like thy wife?
Faust. A plague on her for a hot whore!
Meph. Tut, Faustus,
Marriage is but a ceremonial toy;
And if thou lovest me, think no more of it.
I'll cull thee out the fairest courtesans.
And bring them every morning to thy bed;
She whom thine eye shall like, thy heart
   shall have,
Be she as chaste as was Penelope,
As wise as Saba, or as beautiful
As was bright Lucifer before his fall.
Here, take this book, peruse it thoroughly:
The iterating of these lines brings gold;
The framing of this circle on the ground
Brings whirlwinds, tempests, thunder and
   lightning;
Pronounce this thrice devoutly to thyself,
And men in armour shall appear to thee,
Ready to execute what thou desir'st.
Faust. Thanks, Mephistophilis; yet fain
   would I have a book wherein I might
   behold all spells and incantations, that I
   might raise up spirits when I please.
Meph. Here they are, in this book.
(*Turns to them.*)
Faust. Now would I have a book where I
   might see all characters and planets of
   the heavens, that I might know their mo-
   tions and dispositions.
Meph. Here they are, too.
(*Turns to them.*)
Faust. When I behold the heavens, then I
   repent.
Meph. Why, Faustus,
Thinkest thou Heaven is such a glorious
   thing?

Faustus and Meph. "watch" front center
over audience.
"for a hot whore!" may be cut.

whirlwinds →, tempests, ↑, thunder ↓,
lightning ↑.

I tell thee 'tis not half so fair as thou,
Or any man that breathes on earth.
Faust. How provest thou that?
Meph. 'Twas made for man, therefore is
  man more excellent.
Faust. If it were made for man, 'twas made
  for me;

       (*Enter* GOOD ANGEL *and*
            EVIL ANGEL)
                                              GA and EA enter as they did the first time.

G. Ang. Faustus, repent; yet God will pity
  thee.
E. Ang. Thou art a spirit; God cannot pity
  thee.
Faust. Who buzzeth in mine ears I am a
  spirit?
Be I a devil, yet God may pity me;
Ay, God will pity me if I repent.
E. Ang. Ay, but Faustus never shall repent.   (*Exeunt* ANGELS)
Faust. My heart's so hardened I cannot re-
  pent.
Scarce can I name salvation, faith, or   salvation ↓, faith →, heaven ↑
  heaven,
But fearful echoes thunder in mine ears
"Faustus, thou art damned!"
Faust. Tell me who made the world.
Meph. I will not.
Faust. Sweet Mephistophilis, tell me.
Meph. Move me not, for I will not tell thee.
Faust. Villain, have I not bound thee to tell
  me anything?
Meph. Ay, that is not against our Kingdom;
  but this is.
Think thou on hell, Faustus, for thou art
  damned.
Faust. Think, Faustus, upon God that made
  the world.
Meph. Remember this.
Faust. Ay, go accurséd spirit, to ugly hell.
'Tis thou hast damned distresséd Faustus'
  soul.
Is't not too late?

       (*Re-enter* GOOD ANGEL *and*
            EVIL ANGEL)

E. Ang. Too late.
G. Ang. Never too late, if Faustus can repent.
E. Ang. If thou repent, devils shall tear thee
  in pieces.
G. Ang. Repent, and they shall never raze
  thy skin.

SR spot down, Meph. close one half, Lucifer
and Belzebub enter and stand on either side
of Meph. closed one half, all facing center
stage.

(*Exeunt* ANGELS)

Faust. Ah, Christ, my Savior,
Seek to save distressèd Faustus' soul.

(*Enter* LUCIFER, BELZEBUB, *and* MEPHISTOPHILIS)

Luc. Christ cannot save thy soul, for he is
  just;
There's none but I have interest in the same.
Faust. O, who art thou that look'st so ter-
  rible?
Luc. I am Lucifer,
And this is my companion-prince in hell.
Faust. O Faustus! they are come to fetch
  away thy soul!
Luc. We come to tell thee thou dost injure
  us;
Thou talk'st of Christ contrary to thy prom-
  ise;
Thou should'st not think of God: think of
  the Devil,
and of his dam, too.
Faust. Nor will I henceforth: pardon me
  in this,
And Faustus vows never to look to Heaven,
Never to name God, or to pray to him,
To burn his Scriptures, slay his ministers,
And make my spirits pull his churches
  down.
Luc. Do so, and we will highly gratify thee.
  Faustus, we are come from hell to show
  thee some pastime. Sit down, and thou
  shalt see all the Seven Deadly Sins appear
  in their proper shapes.
Faust. That sight will be pleasing unto me,
As Paradise was to Adam the first day
Of his creation.
Luc. Talk not of Paradise nor creation, but
  mark this show: talk of the Devil and
  nothing else.—Come away.

(*Enter the* SEVEN DEADLY SINS)

Now, Faustus, examine them of their several
  names and dispositions.
Faust. What art thou—the first?
Pride. I am Pride. I disdain to have
  any parents. I am like to Ovid's flea: I
  can creep into every corner of a wench;
  sometimes, like a periwig, I set upon his
  brow; or like a fan of feathers, I kiss his
  lips; indeed I do—what do I not? But, fie,

Angels exeunt.

Lucifer, Belzebub, and Meph. open full.
Meph. seated, Luc. and Bel. on either side
standing.

Lights dim and sins enter. Use seven spots.
Each fades in as "sin" speaks.
1. under small ladder, sitting, head and feet
   up. (Sloth)
2. standing on small ladder with feet on
   two levels. (Pride)

(proudly)

3. sitting on top of steps center. (Wrath)
4. leaning against steps. (Gluttony)
5. standing on stage floor with one foot up
   on ladder. (Envy)

what a scent is here! I'll not speak another word, except the ground were perfumed, and covered with cloth of arras.

Faust. What art thou—the second?

Covet. I am Covetousness, begotten of an old churl in an old lethern bag; and might I have my wish I would desire that this house and all the people in it were turned to gold, that I might lock you up in my good chest. O, my sweet gold!

Faust. What art thou—the third?

Wrath. I am Wrath. I had neither father nor mother: I leapt out of a lion's mouth when I was scarce half an hour old; and ever since I have run up and down the world with this case of rapiers wounding myself when I had nobody to fight withal. I was born in hell; and look to it, for some of you shall be my father.

Faust. What art thou—the fourth?

Envy. I am Envy, begotten of a chimney sweeper and an oysterwife. I cannot read, and therefore wish all books were burnt. I am lean with seeing others eat. O that there would come a famine through all the world, that all might die, and I live alone! then thou should'st see how fat I would be. But must thou sit and I stand! Come down with a vengeance!

Faust. Away, envious rascal! What art thou —the fifth?

Glut. Who, I, sir? I am Gluttony. My parents are dead, and the devil a penny they have left me, but a bare pension, and that is thirty meals a day and ten bevers—a small trifle to suffice nature. O, I come of royal parentage! My grandfather was a Gammon of Bacon, my grandmother a Hogshead of Claret-wine; my godfathers were these, Peter Pickleherring, and Martin Martlesmas-beef. O, but my godmother, she was a jolly gentlewoman, and well beloved in every good town and city; her name was Mistress Margery Marchbeer. Now, Faustus, thou hast heard all my progeny, wilt thou bid me to supper?

Faust. No, I'll see thee hanged: thou wilt eat up all my victuals.

Glut. Then the Devil choke thee!

Faust. Choke thyself, glutton! Who art thou —the sixth?

6. standing on first step of large ladder. (Covetousness)
7. sitting on top of large ladder, one foot handing downstage, the other on a ladder step. (Lechery)

(sneeringly)

(hatefully)

("case" means pair.)

(whining)

(smack lips)

("bevers" means refreshments between meals.)

Sloth. I am Sloth. I was begotten on a sunny bank, where I have lain ever since; and you have done me great injury to bring me from thence: let me be carried thither again by Gluttony and Lechery. I'll not speak another word for a king's ransom.

(sleepily)

Faust. What are you, Mistress Minx, the seventh and last?

Lech. Who, I, sir? I am one that loves an inch of raw mutton better than an ell of fried stockfish; and the first letter of my name begins with Lechery.

(sneeringly)

Luc. Away to hell, to hell! (*Exeunt the* SINS)—Now, Faustus, how dost thou like this?

Faust. O, this feeds my soul!

Luc. Tut, Faustus, in hell is all manner of delight.

Faust. O might I see hell, and return again. How happy were I then!

Luc. Thou shalt; I will send for thee at midnight.

In meantime take this book; peruse it thoroughly,

And thou shalt turn thyself into what shape thou wilt.

Faust. Great thanks, mighty Lucifer!
This will I keep as chary as my life.

Luc. Farewell, Faustus, and think on the Devil.

Faust. Farewell, great Lucifer! Come, Mephistophilis.

(*Exeunt omnes*)

(*Enter* WAGNER)

Wagner. Learnéd Faustus,
To know the secrets of astronomy,
Graven in the book of Jove's high firmament,
Did mount himself to scale Olympus' top,
Being seated in a chariot burning bright,
Drawn by the strength of yoky dragons' necks.
He now is gone to prove cosmography,
And, as I guess, will first arrive at Rome,
To see the Pope and manner of his court,
And take some part of holy Peter's feast,
That to this day is highly solemnised.

(*Exit*)

Dim lights as exeunt.

PART II

We felt an intermission was necessary for two reasons: (1) this was a new experience for our audience, and discussion of what they had seen in Part I was beneficial, (2) the readers needed ten minutes to rejuvenate themselves.

Wagner steps on stage just down from Faustus' stool and remains standing.

Wagner exits.

SCENE VII (*The* POPE'S *Privy Chamber.*)

(*Enter* FAUSTUS *and*
MEPHISTOPHILIS)

Faust. Hast thou, as erst I did command,
Conducted me within the walls of Rome?
Meph. Faustus, I have; and because we will
    not be unprovided, I have taken up his
    Holiness' privy-chamber for our use.
Faust. I hope his Holiness will bid us wel-
    come.
Meph. Tut, 'tis no matter, man, we'll be bold
    with his good cheer.
Faust. Now by the kingdoms of infernal rule,
Of Styx, of Acheron, and the fiery lake
Of ever-burning Phlegethon, I swear
That I do long to see the monuments
And situation of bright-splendent Rome:
Come therefore, let's away.
Meph. Nay, Faustus, stay; I know you'd fain
    see the Pope,
And take some part of holy Peter's feast,
Where thou shalt see a troop of bald-pate
    friars,
Whose *summum bonum* is in belly-cheer.
Faust. Well, I'm content to compass then
    some sport,
And by their folly make us merriment.
Then charm me, (Mephistophilis,) that I
May be invisible, to do what I please
Unseen of any whilst I stay in Rome.

(MEPHISTOPHILIS *charms him.*)

Meph. So, Faustus, now
Do what thou wilt, thou shalt not be dis-
    cerned.

(*Sound a sennet. Enter the* POPE *and the*
CARDINAL *of* LORRAIN *to the banquet,*
    with FRIARS *attending.*)

Pope. My Lord of Lorrain, wilt please you
    draw near?
Faust. Fall to, and the devil choke you!
Pope. How now! Who's that which spake?
    Friars, look about.
I Friar. Here's nobody, if it like your Holi-
    ness.
Pope. My lord, here is a dainty dish was
    sent me from the Bishop of Milan.
Faust. I thank you, sir.

(Typical church organ music sets the
mood.)

Faustus takes his stool SL.
Meph. takes his stool SR.

"Rome" and "his Holiness' privy-chamber"
are very important. As in Shakespeare, they
set the scene when there is no stage set.

Meph. crosses to Faustus.

Pope takes Meph. stool, Friar to his right,
and Cardinal to his left.

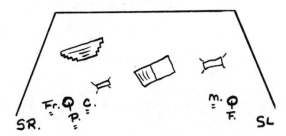

(*Snatches it.*)

Pope. How now! Who's that which snatched the meat from me? Will no man look? My Lord, this dish was sent me from the Cardinal of Florence.

Faust. You say true; I'll ha't

(*Snatches it.*)

Pope. My lord, I'll drink to your Grace.

Faust. I'll pledge your Grace.

(*Snatches the cup.*)

C. of Lor. My lord, it may be some ghost newly crept out of purgatory, come to beg a pardon of your Holiness.

Pope. It may be so. Friars, prepare a dirge to lay the fury of this ghost.

(*The* POPE *crosses Himself, and* FAUSTUS *hits him a box on the ear.*)

Come on, Mephistophilis, what shall we do?

Meph. Nay, I know not. We shall be cursed with bell, book, and candle.

Faust. How! bell, book, and candle,—candle, book, and bell, Forward and backward to curse Faustus to hell!

Anon you shall hear a hog grunt, a calf bleat, and an ass bray,

Because it is Saint Peter's holiday.

(*Re-enter all the* FRIARS *to sing the Dirge*)

I Friar. Come, brethren, let's about our business with good devotion.

(*They sing:*)

Cursed be he that stole away his Holiness' meat from the table!

Maledicat Dominus!

Cursed be he that struck his Holiness a blow on the face!

Maledicat Dominus!

Cursed be he that took Friar Sandelo a blow on the pate!

Maledicat Dominus!

Cursed be he that disturbeth our holy dirge!

Maledicat Dominus! Et omnes sancti! Amen!

Read with force and a slightly delayed upward jerk of script.

Same as above.

Same as above.

Chorus may enter in darkness to risers. We had them simulate a processional from SL across behind Meph. and Faustus to the risers.

(S) Solo
If chorus enters in darkness, the lights come up on them as they begin to sing.
(A) If they move in a processional, the riser lights come up after the first two or three take their places on the risers.
(S)

(A)
(S)

(A)
(S)
(A)

(MEPHISTOPHILIS *and* FAUSTUS *beat the* FRIARS, *and fling fireworks among them: and so exeunt*)

Lights blackout.
Friar, Cardinal, Pope exeunt.

(*Enter* CHORUS)

Lights on chorus up full.

Chorus. When Faustus had with pleasure ta'en the view
Of rarest things, and royal courts of kings,
He stayed his course, and so returnéd home;
Where such as bear his absence but with grief,
I mean his friends, and near'st companions,
Did gratulate his safety with kind words,
And in their conference of what befell,
Touching his journey through the world and air,
They put forth questions of Astrology,
Which Faustus answered with such learnéd skill,
As they admired and wondered at his wit.

Chorus must display change from Friars to narrators.

Meph. and Faustus relax, turn one quarter closed.

Lights on chorus dim to blackout.

SCENE XII (*Court of the* DUKE)

(*Enter the* DUKE *of* VANHOLT, *the* DUCHESS, FAUSTUS, *and* MEPHIS-TOPHILIS)

Duchess sits on SL stool.
Duke stands slightly behind and to her right.

Duke. Believe me, Master Doctor, this merriment hath much pleased me.

Faust. My gracious lord, I am glad it contents you so well.—But it may be, madam, you take no delight in this. I have heard that great-bellied women do long for some dainties or other. What is it, madam? Tell me, and you shall have it.

Duchess. Thanks, good Master Doctor; and for I see your courteous intent to pleasure me, I will not hide from you the thing my heart desires; and were it now summer, as it is January and the dead time of winter, I would desire no better meat than a dish of ripe grapes.

Faust. Alas, madam, that's nothing! Mephistophilis, begone. (*Exit* MEPHISTOPH-ILIS) Were it a greater thing than this, so it would content you, you should have it.

Meph. close one quarter.

(*Re-enter* MEPHISTOPHILIS *with the grapes*)

Meph. open full.

Here they be, madam; wilt please you taste on them?

Hand out front, palm up.

Duchess. Believe me, Master Doctor, they be the best grapes that e'er I tasted in my life before.

Faust. I am glad they content you so, madam.

Duke. Come, madam, let us in, where you must reward this learnéd man for the great kindness he hath showed to you.

Duchess. And so I will, my lord; and whilst I live, rest beholding for this courtesy.

Faust. I humbly thank your Grace.

Duke. Come, Master Doctor, follow us and receive your reward.

(*Exeunt*)   Duke and Duchess exit. SR spots dim.

(*Enter* CHORUS)   Lights up on chorus.

Chorus. Now is his fame spread forth in every land;   Faustus close one quarter.
Amongst the rest the Emperor is one,
Carolus the Fifth, at whose palace now
Faustus is feasted 'mongst his noblemen.

(*Exit*)

SCENE X. (*The* EMPEROR'S *Court*)

(*Enter* EMPEROR, FAUSTUS, *and a* KNIGHT *with attendants*)   Emperor sits SR stool. Knight stands to his side. SR spots up.

Emp. Master Doctor Faustus, I have heard strange report of thy knowledge in the black art, how that none in my empire nor in the whole world can compare with thee for the rare effects of magic; they say thou hast a familiar spirit, by whom thou canst accomplish what thou list. This, therefore, is my request, that thou let me see some proof of thy skill, that mine eyes may be witnesses to confirm what mine ears have heard reported; and here I swear to thee by the honour of mine imperial crown, that, whatever thou doest, thou shalt be no ways prejudiced or endamaged.   Faustus open full.

Knight. (Aside.) I' faith he looks much like a conjuror.

Faust. My gracious sovereign, though I must confess myself far inferior to the report men have published, and nothing answerable to the honour of your imperial majesty, yet for that love and duty binds me thereunto, I am content to do whatsoever your majesty shall command me.

Emp. Then, Doctor Faustus, mark what I
  shall say.
As I was sometime solitary set
Within my closet, sundry thoughts arose
About the honour of my ancestors,
How they had won by prowess such exploits,
Got such riches, subdued so many king-
  doms,
As we that do succeed, or they that shall
Hereafter possess our throne, shall
(I fear me) ne'er attain to that degree
Of high renown and great authority;
Amongst which kings is Alexander the
  Great,
Chief spectacle of the world's pre-eminence,
The bright shining of whose glorious acts
Lightens the world with his reflecting beams,
As, when I heard but mention made of him,
It grieves my soul I never saw the man.
If, therefore, thou by cunning of thy art
Canst raise this man from hollow vaults
  below,
Where lies entombed this famous conqueror,
And bring with him his beauteous para-
  mour,
Both in their right shapes, gesture, and attire
They used to wear during their time of life,
Thou shalt both satisfy my just desire,
And give me cause to praise thee whilst I
  live.
Faust. My gracious lord, I am ready to
  accomplish your request so far forth as
  by art, and power of my Spirit, I am able
  to perform.
Knight. (*Aside.*) I' faith that's just nothing
  at all.
Faust. But, if it like your Grace, it is not
  in my ability to present before your eyes
  the true substantial bodies of those two
  deceased princes, which long since are
  consumed to dust.
Knight. (*Aside.*) Ay, merry, Master Doctor,
  now there's a sign of grace in you, when
  you will confess the truth.
Faust. But such spirits as can lively resemble
  Alexander and his paramour shall appear
  before your Grace in that manner that
  they best lived in, in their most flourish-
  ing estate; which I doubt not shall suffi-
  ciently content your imperial majesty.
Emp. Go to, Master Doctor, let me see them
  presently.

Knight. Do you hear, Master Doctor? You bring Alexander and his paramour before the Emperor!

Faust. How then, sir?

Knight. I' faith that's as true as Diana turned me to a stag!

Faust. No, sir, but when Actaeon died, he left the horns for you. Mephistophilis, begone. (*Exit* MEPHIS-TOPHILIS)

Meph. close one quarter.

Knight. Nay, an you go to conjuring, I'll begone.

Knight close one quarter.

(*Exit*)

Faust. I'll meet with you anon for interrupting me so. Here they are, my gracious lord.

(*Re-enter* MEPHISTOPHILIS *with* SPIR-ITS *in the shape of* ALEXANDER *and his* PARAMOUR)

Meph. open full.
No added characters. We used them and they were not needed and only served to draw undue attention to themselves.

Emp. Master Doctor, I heard this lady while she lived had a wart or mole on her neck: How shall I know whether it be so or not?

Faust. Your Highness may boldly go and see.

(*Exeunt* SPIRITS)

Emp. Sure these are no spirits, but true substantial bodies of those two deceased princes.

Faust. Will't please your Highness now to send for that knight that was so pleasant with me here of late?

Emp. One of you call him forth.

(*Exit* Attendant)

(*Re-enter the* KNIGHT *with a pair of horns on his head*)

Knight open full, head up.

How now, sir knight! why I had thought thou had'st been a bachelor, but now I see thou hast a wife, that not only gives thee horns, but makes thee wear them. Feel on thy head.

Knight. Thou damned wretch and execrable dog,
Bred in the concave of some monstrous rock,
How darest thou thus abuse a gentleman?
Villain, I say, undo what thou hast done!

Feel head and "horns."

Faust. O, not so fast, sir; there's no haste; but, good, are you remembered how you crossed me in my conference with you for it.

Emp. Good Master Doctor, at my entreaty release him; he hath done penance sufficient.

Faust. My gracious lord, not so much for the injury he offered me here in your presence, as to delight you with some mirth, hath Faustus worthily requited this injurious knight; which, being all I desire, I am content to release him of his horns: and, sir knight, hereafter speak well of scholars. Mephistophilis, transform him straight. (MEPHISTOPHILIS removes the horns) Now, my good lord, having done my duty I humbly take my leave.

Emp. Farewell, Master Doctor; yet, ere you go,

Expect from me a bounteous reward.

(*Exeunt*)

All but Faustus and Meph. exit.

SCENE XI. (*A Green, then the House of* FAUSTUS)

(*Enter* FAUSTUS *and* MEPHISTOPHILIS)

Faust. Now, Mephistophilis, the restless course
That Time doth run with calm and silent foot,
Short'ning my days and thread of vital life,
Calls for the payment of my latest years;
Therefore, sweet Mephistophilis, let us
Make haste to Wittenberg.

Faustus close one quarter.

SCENE XIII. (*A Room in the House of* FAUSTUS)

(*Enter* WAGNER, *solus*)

Wagner in SR.

Wag. I think my master means to die shortly,
For he hath given to me all his goods;
And yet, methinks, if that death were near,
He would not banquet and carouse and swill
Amongst the students, as even now he doth,
Who are at supper with such belly-cheer
As Wagner ne'er beheld in all his life.
See where they come! Belike the feast is ended.

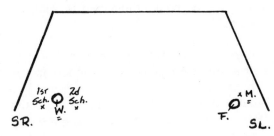

(*Enter* FAUSTUS, *with two or three* SCHOLARS *and* MEPHISTOPHILIS)

Scholars in on either side of Wagner.

1 Schol. Master Doctor Faustus, since our conference about fair ladies, which was

the beautifullest in all the world, we have
determined with ourselves that Helen of
Greece was the admirablest lady that ever
lived: therefore, Master Doctor, if you
will do us that favour, as to let us see
that peerless dame of Greece, whom all
the world admires for majesty, we should
think ourselves much beholding unto you.

Faust. Gentlemen,
For that I know your friendship is un-
  feigned,
And Faustus' custom is not to deny
The just requests of those that wish him well,
You shall behold that peerless dame of
  Greece,
No otherways for pomp and majesty
Than when Sir Paris crossed the seas with
  her,
And brought the spoils to rich Dardania.
Be silent, then, for danger is in words.

(*Music sounds, and* HELEN *passeth over
the stage*)   (Music ad lib.) No "Helen."

1 Schol. Since we have seen the pride of
  Nature's works
And only paragon of excellence,
Let us depart; and for this glorious deed
Happy and blest be Faustus evermore.
Faust. Gentlemen, farewell—the same I
  wish to you.

(*Exeunt* SCHOLARS *and* WAGNER)
                                              Exeunt stage R.

Where art thou, Faustus? Wretch, what has
  thou done?   All lights dim except on SL on Faustus.
Damned art thou, Faustus, damned; despair
  and die!
Hell calls for right, and with a roaring voice   Meph. cross to SR in darkness take SR stool.
Says "Faustus! come! thine hour is (*almost*)
  come!"

I do repent; and yet I do despair;
Hell strives with grace for conquest in my
  breast:
What shall I do to shun the snares of death?
Meph. Thou traitor, Faustus, I arrest thy   SR spot up on Meph.
  soul
For disobedience to my sovereign lord;
Revolt, and I'll in piecemeal tear thy flesh.
Faust. Sweet Mephistophilis, entreat thy lord
To pardon my unjust presumption,

And with my blood again I will confirm
My former vow I made to Lucifer.
Meph. Do it then quickly, with unfeigned
    heart,
Lest greater danger do attend thy drift.
Faust. One thing, good servant, let me crave
    of thee,
To glut the longing of my heart's desire,—
That I might have unto my paramour
That heavenly Helen, which I saw of late,
Whose sweet embracings may extinguish
    clean
These thoughts that do dissuade me from
    my vow,
And keep mine oath I made to Lucifer.
Meph. Faustus, this and what else thou shalt
    desire
Shall be performed in twinkling of an eye.

      (*Re-enter* HELEN)

Faust. Was this the face that launched a
    thousand ships
And burnt the topless towers of Ilium?
Sweet Helen, make me immortal with a kiss.
(*Kisses her.*) Her lips suck forth my soul;
    see where it flies!—
Come, Helen, come, give me my soul again.
Here will I dwell, for Heaven in these lips,
And all is dross that is not Helen.
I will be Paris, and for love of thee,
Instead of Troy, shall Wittenberg be sacked;
And I will combat with weak Menelaus,
And wear thy colours on my pluméd crest;
Yea, I will wound Achilles in the heel,
And then return to Helen for a kiss.
Oh, thou art fairer than the evening air
Clad in the beauty of a thousand stars;
Brighter art thou than flaming Jupiter
When he appeared to hapless Semele:
More lovely than the monarch of the sky
In wanton Arethusa's azured arms:
And none but thou shalt be my paramour.

      (*Exeunt*)

    SCENE XIV (*The Same*)

(*Enter* FAUSTUS *with the* SCHOLARS)

Faust. Ah, gentlemen!
1 Schol. What ails Faustus?
Faust. Ah, my sweet chamber-fellow, had I

Faustus looks up and out.
Helen does not appear.

Faustus focus out from stage and above
audience into space.

Memorize speech.

No exit.

Scholars in left and stand on either side of
Faustus.

lived with thee then had I lived still! but now I die eternally. Look, comes he not, comes he not?

2 Schol. What means Faustus?

3 Schol. Belike he is grown into some sickness by being over solitary.

1 Schol. If it be so, we'll have physicians to cure him. 'Tis but a surfeit. Never fear, man.

Faust. A surfeit of deadly sin that hath damned both body and soul.

2 Schol. Yet, Faustus, look up to Heaven; remember God's mercies are infinite.

Faust. But Faustus' offences can never be pardoned: the serpent that tempted Eve may be saved, but not Faustus. Ah, gentlemen, hear me with patience, and tremble not at my speeches! Though my heart pants and quivers to remember that I have been a student here these thirty years, oh, would that I had never seen Wittenberg, never read book! And what wonders I have done, all Germany can witness, yea, all the world; for which Faustus hath lost both Germany and the world, yea Heaven itself, Heaven, the seat of God, the throne of the blessèd, the kingdom of joy; and must remain in hell for ever, hell. Sweet friends! What shall become of Faustus being in hell for ever?

3 Schol. Yet, Faustus, call on God.

Faust. On God, whom Faustus hath abjured! on God, whom Faustus hath blasphemed! Ah, my God, I would weep, but the Devil draws in my tears. Gush forth blood instead of tears! Yea, life and soul! Oh, he stays my tongue! I would lift up my hands, but see, they hold them, they hold them!

All. Who, Faustus?

Faust. Lucifer and Mephistophilis. Ah, gentlemen, I gave them my soul for my cunning!

All. God forbid!

Faust. God forbade it indeed; but Faustus hath done it. For vain pleasure of twenty-four years hath Faustus lost eternal joy and felicity. I writ them a bill with mine own blood: the date is expired; the time will come, and he will fetch me.

1 Schol. Why did not Faustus tell us of this

before, that divines might have prayed for thee?

Faust. Oft have I thought to have done so; but the Devil threatened to tear me in pieces if I named God; to fetch both body and soul if I once gave ear to divinity: and now 'tis too late. Gentlemen, away! lest you perish with me.

2 Schol. Oh, what shall we do to save Faustus?

Faust. Talk not of me, but save yourselves, and depart.

3 Schol. God will strengthen me. I will stay with Faustus.

1 Schol. Tempt not God, sweet friend; but let us into the next room, and there pray for him.

Faust. Ay, pray for me, pray for me! and what noise soever ye hear, come not unto me, for nothing can rescue me.

2 Schol. Pray thou, and we will pray that God may have mercy upon thee.

Faust. Gentlemen, farewell! If I live till morning I'll visit you: if not—Faustus is gone to hell.

All. Faustus, farewell!

(*Exeunt* SCHOLARS. *The clock strikes eleven.*)

Scholars exit.
Clock strikes.
Lights out except SL spot on Faustus.

Faust. Ah, Faustus,
Now hast thou but one bare hour to live,
And then thou must be damned perpetually!
Stand still, you ever-moving spheres of Heaven,
That time may cease, and midnight never come;
Fair Nature's eye, rise, rise again and make
Perpetual day; or let this hour be but
A year, a month, a week, a natural day,
That Faustus may repent and save his soul!
O lente, lente currite noctis equi!
The stars move still, time runs, the clock will strike,
The Devil will come, and Faustus must be damned.
O, I'll leap up to my God! Who pulls me down?
See, see where Christ's blood streams in the firmament!
One drop would save my soul—half a drop: Ah, my Christ!

Ah, rend not my heart for naming of my
  Christ!
Yet will I call on him: O spare me, Luci-
  fer!—
Where is it now? 'Tis gone; and see where
  God
Stretcheth out his arm, and bends his ireful
  brows!
Mountain and hill come, come and fall on
  me,
And hide me from the heavy wrath of God!
No! No!
Then will I headlong run into the earth;
Earth gape! O no, it will not harbour me!
You stars that reigned at my nativity,
Whose influence hath allotted death and
  hell,
Now draw up Faustus like a foggy mist
Into the entrails of yon labouring cloud,
That when they vomit forth into the air,
My limbs may issue from your smoky
  mouths,
So that my soul may but ascend to Heaven.

(*The watch strikes the half hour.*)   Clock strikes.

Ah, half the hour is past! 'Twill all be past
  anon!
O God!   Chorus on to risers slowly and in darkness.
If thou wilt not have mercy on my soul,   Caution groups to keep in complete charac-
Yet for Christ's sake whose blood hath   ter in darkness. Undue movement *can* be
  ransomed me,   seen.
Impose some end to my incessant pain;
Let Faustus live in hell a thousand years—
A hundred thousand, and at last be saved!
O, no end is limited to damned souls!
Why wert thou not a creature wanting soul?
Or why is this immortal that that thou hast?
Ah, Pythagoras' metempsychosis! were that
  true,
This soul should fly from me, and I be
  changed
Unto some brutish beast! All beasts are
  happy,
For, when they die,
Their souls are soon dissolved in elements;
But mine must live, still to be plagued in
  hell.
Curst be the parents that engendered me!
No, Faustus: curse thyself: curse Lucifer
That hath deprived thee of the joys of
  Heaven.

(*The clock striketh twelve.*)   Clock strikes.

O, it strikes, it strikes! Now, body, turn to
    air,
Or Lucifer will bear thee quick to hell.

      (*Thunder and lightning*)   (thunder)

O soul, be changed into little water-drops,
And fall into the ocean—ne'er be found.
My God! my God! look not so fierce on me!

        (*Enter* DEVILS)

Adders and serpents, let me breathe awhile!
Ugly hell, gape not! come not, Lucifer!
I'll burn my books!—Ah Mephistophilis!

Here is where we used the flash box for the smoke effect.

   (*Exeunt* DEVILS *with* FAUSTUS)

      (*Enter* CHORUS)

Rather, Faustus drop head and turn three quarters to full closed. Lights down SL.

(*Cho.*) Cut is the branch that might have
    grown full straight,
And burned is Apollo's laurel bough,
That sometimes grew within this learnéd
    man.
Faustus is gone; regard his hellish fall,
Whose fiendful fortune may exhort the wise
Only to wonder at unlawful things,
Whose deepness doth entice such forward
    wits
To practise more than heavenly power per-
    mits.

Lights up on chorus.

         (*Exit*)

MENAECHMI
or THE TWO MENAECHMUSES

By Plautus

Translated by Paul Nixon

CHARACTERS

Peniculus, a parasite
Menaechmus, a young gentleman living in Epidamnus
Menaechmus (Sosicles), a young gentleman of Syracuse
Erotium, a courtesan
Cylindrus, her cook
Messenio, slave of Menaechmus (Sosicles)
Maid, in the service of Erotium
Wife of Menaechmus
Father-in-law of Menaechmus
A doctor

Scene—Epidamnus. A street in which stand the houses of Menaechmus and Erotium.

ARGUMENT

A Sicilian merchant, who had twin sons, died after one of them had been stolen. To the boy who was left at home his paternal grandfather gave the name of the stolen brother, calling him Menaechmus instead of Sosicles. And this boy, after he grew up, began searching for his brother in every land. At last he comes to Epidamnus: here it was that his stolen brother had been brought up. Everyone takes the stranger for their own fellow citizen Menaechmus, and he is so addressed by his brother's mistress, wife, and father-in-law. At last the brothers recognise each other.

PROLOGUE

First and foremost, spectators, I am the bearer of the very best wishes for—myself and—you. I bring you Plautus, orally, not corporally, and I pray you receive him with amiable ears. Lend me your attention and learn our argument now; I will frame it in the fewest possible words.

The Menaechmi is an example of very confusing material when lateral (parallel) movement is not employed.

Twins would be fun to use and *can be* since both are within audience view throughout.

A narrator is used for the Argument and the Prologue.

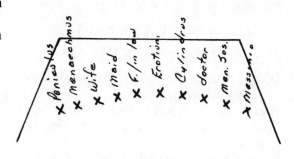

Readers enter. Boys' scripts are in the right hand hanging at arm's length. Girls' scripts are held in the right hand with the arm crooked.

Narrator (DSC)

Narrator (moves SL) change to plural: "We are. . . ."

Now writers of comedy have this habit: they always allege that the scene of action is Athens, their object being to give the play a more Grecian air. As for me, I will report the scene as being nowhere, save where, by report, the events occurred. And though this argument is à la Greek, yet it is not à l'Attic but rather à la Sicilian. So much by way of antelude to this argument; now I will give you your rations of the argument itself, not by the peck or three-peck measure, but by the very granary—such is my generosity in giving arguments!

Cut: "Now writers . . . arguments!" ***

There was a certain old merchant in Syracuse who had twin sons born him, so much alike that their foster mother who suckled them could not distinguish them, nor even their real mother who gave them birth—so I was told, at least, by a man who had seen the boys; I myself have not seen them, and none of you is to suppose I have. When the boys were now seven years old, their father loaded a large ship with many articles of merchandise; one twin he put aboard and took away with himself to Tarentum, his place of trade, the other being left with his mother at home. At Tarentum it happened they were having a festival when he arrived. Many people had congregated, as they do at festivals; the boy strayed from his father in the crowd. A certain merchant of Epidamnus was there; this merchant picked the boy up and took him off to Epidamnus. As for the father, after he lost his son he was broken-hearted and died of grief at Tarentum a few days later.

***

When news of all this—how the boy was stolen and his father dead at Tarentum—got back to Syracuse to the boy's grandfather, he changed the name of this other twin. See what a deep affection he had for the other boy, the stolen one! He gave that boy's name to the one at home, calling him Menaechmus, the name of his lost brother. This was the name of the grandfather himself, too,—(*confidentially*) I remember his name the more easily for having seen him vociferously dunned. To keep you from going astray later, I herewith forewarn you—both twins have the same name.

Now I must (*chuckling*) foot it back to Epidamnus so as to clarify this situation for

Narrator (cut: "Now I must . . . However," ***

you perfectly. If any one of you should want any business transacted for him in Epidamnus, command me freely and speak out —that is, in case you furnish the wherewithal for the transaction. For if a man has not furnished the necessary funds, it will come to nothing; if he has furnished them, it will come to—less than nothing. However, I return to the place I left, yes, and without stirring a step.

That Epidamnian I mentioned some time ago, who stole that other twin, had no children at all except his money. He adopted that kidnapped boy and gave him a wife with a dowry, and made him his heir by his own demise. For he happened one day to be going to the country after a heavy rain, and while he was trying to ford a rapid stream quite near the city, the rapids rapt the feet of the boy's abductor from beneath him and swept him off to perdition. His enormous fortune fell to his adopted son. And there it is (*pointing to house*) that this stolen twin lives.

Now that twin whose home is in Syracuse will come to-day to Epidamnus, with his servant, in search of this twin brother of his. This city (*with a wave toward the houses on the stage*) is Epidamnus, during the presentation of this play; when another play is presented it will become another town. It is quite like the way in which families, too, are wont to change their homes: now a pimp lives here, now a young gentleman, now an old one, now a poor man, a beggar, a king, a parasite, a seer.

***

ACT I

SCENE I

(*Enter Peniculus, looking dejected*)

Pen. The young fellows have given me the name of Brush,[1] the reason being that when I eat I sweep the table clean. (*with fervor*) Men that bind prisoners of war with chains and fasten shackles on runaway slaves are awful fools, at least in my opinion. Why, if the poor devil has this extra trouble on his shoulders, too, he's all the

[1] The meaning of Peniculus.

Peniculus enjoys all of his own remarks with the audience.

Peniculus stands, removes DSR.

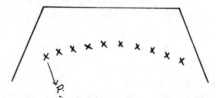

Peniculus cut: "Men that . . . they cling."
***

keener for escape and mischief. Why, they get out of their chains somehow. As for those in shackles, they file away the ring, or knock the rivet off with a stone. Nonsensical measures! The man you really want to keep from running off ought to be bound with (*sighing*) food and drink. A loaded table—(*smacking his lips*) tie his snout to that! Just you deal him our meat and drink to suit his pleasure and his appetite each day, and he'll never run—Lord, no!—no matter if he's done a deed for hanging. You'll keep him easily so long as you bind him with these bonds. They're such extraordinarily tenacious bonds, these bellybands: the more you stretch 'em, the closer they cling. Here's my case—I'm going to Menaechmus here (*pointing to house*), whose bond servant I've been for many a day, going of my own accord to let him bind me. Why, (*enthusiastically*) that man doesn't merely feed men, he nurtures them and re-creates them; a better doctor can't be found. Here's the sort of young fellow he is: a splendid trencherman himself, he gives you dinners fit for the festival of Ceres; piles up the courses so, erects such heaps of lovely panny things, you must stand on your couch if you want anything from off the top. (*pauses, then sadly*) But for now these many days there has been a gap in my invitations; and all this time I've kept fast at home with my (*lingeringly*) dear ones. For not a thing do I eat or buy that isn't, oh, so dear! And now another point is—these dears I've marshalled are deserting me. (*looking towards Menaechmus's house*) So here's for a call on him. But the door's opening! Aha! I see Menaechmus himself! He's coming out! (*steps back*)

***

Peniculus steps right and back.

Scene II

(*Enter Menaechmus, followed to the doorway by his wife*)

Men. (*angrily*) If you weren't mean, if you weren't stupid, if you weren't a violent virago, what you see displeases your husband would be displeasing to you, too. Now mark my words, if you act like this toward me after to-day, you shall hie yourself home to your father as a divorcee. Why, when-

Menaechmus stands, moves DSR.

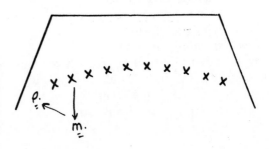

ever I want to go out, you catch hold of me, call me back, cross-question me as to where I'm going, what I'm doing, what business I have in hand, what I'm after, what I've got, what I did when I was out. I've married a custom-house officer, judging from the way everything—all I've done and am doing—must be declared. I've pampered you too much; now then, I'll state my future policy. Inasmuch as I keep you well provided with maids, food, woollen cloth, jewellery, coverlets, purple dresses, and you lack for nothing, you (*with emphasis*) will look out for trouble if you're wise, and cease spying on your husband. (*in lower tone as his wife goes back inside*) And furthermore, that you may not watch me for nothing, I'll reward your diligence by taking a wench to dinner and inviting myself out somewhere.

Pen. (*aside, mournfully*) The fellow pretends to be abusing his wife, when he is abusing me; for if he dines out, it's certainly me, not his wife, he punishes.

Men. (*elated*) Hurrah! By Jove, at last my lecture has driven her away from the door! Where are your married gallants? Why don't they all hurry up with gifts and congratulations for my valiant fight? (*showing a woman's mantle worn underneath his cloak*) This mantle I just now stole from my wife inside there, and (*gleefully*) it's going to a wench. This is the way to do—to cheat a cunning gaoler in such clever style! Ah, this is a beautiful job, a handsome job, a neat job, a workmanlike job! I've done the wretch out of this—(*dryly*) and done myself, too!—and it's on the road to (*glancing at Erotium's house*) ruin. (*pauses, then cheerfully*) I have taken booty from the enemy without loss to my allies.

Pen. (*loudly, from his retreat*) Hi, sir! Is there some share in that booty for me?

Men. (*startled and covering mantle again*) Good Lord! Detected!

Pen. Oh no, protected! Never fear!

Men. Who goes there?

Pen. (*stepping forward*) I.

Men. (*vastly relieved*) Ah there, old Timeliness! Ah there, old Opportunity! Good day! (*extends his hand*)

Pen. (*taking it*) Good day, sir.

Peniculus moves down again and right to Menaechmus.

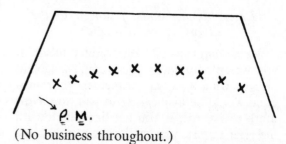

(No business throughout.)

Men. And what are you doing with your-self?

Pen. Shaking hands with my guardian angel.

Men. You couldn't have arrived at a more fitting time for me.

Pen. A habit of mine; I know every juncture of timeliness.

Men. Do you want to set your eyes on a rich treat?

Pen. What cook cooked it? I shall know if there has been a culinary slip as soon as I see the leavings.

Cut: "I shall . . . with me." ***

Men. Tell me, have you ever seen a wall painting showing the eagle making off with Catamitus[2] or Venus with Adonis?

Pen. Often. But what have such pictures got to do with me?

***

Men. (*revealing the mantle*) Come, cast your eye on me. Do I look at all like them?

Pen. What sort of a get-up is that?

Men. Say that I'm a splendid fellow.

Pen. (*suspiciously*) What are we going to eat?

Men. Just you say what I command.

Pen. (*listlessly*) I do—splendid fellow.

Men. Won't you add something of your own?

Pen. (*with a sigh*) The jolliest sort of fellow, too.

Men. Go on, go on!

Pen. (*indignant*) By gad, I will not go on, without knowing what good it does me. You and your wife are at odds, so I am on my guard against you all the more guardedly.

Men. (*reassuringly*) But there's a place she's unaware of, where we can have a beautiful time and fairly burn up this day.

Pen. (*eagerly*) Come, come, then, by all means! fairly spoken! Now how soon shall I kindle the pyre? Why, the day is half dead already, dead down to its navel.

Men. You delay yourself by interrupting me.

Pen. Knock my eye clean through its socket, Menaechmus, if I utter a single word —without your orders.

---

[2] Ganymede, carried off to Jupiter.

Men. (*edging away from his house*) Come over here away from the door.

Pen. (*obeying*) All right.

Men. (*elaborately cautious*) Here, still farther.

Pen. Very well.

Men. (*still retreating*) Be a man—come still farther from that lioness's lair.

Pen. (*laughing*) Bravo! Gad, you certainly would make a fine charioteer, I do believe.

Men. Why so?

Pen. You look back so often to make sure your wife is not catching up with you.

Men. But what do you say—

Pen. I? Why, whatever you want—that's what I say and unsay.

Men. If you happened to smell something, would the odour enable you to conjecture?   Cut: "If you happened . . . you have" ***

Pen. The Board of Augurs should be consulted.

Men. (*holding out the lower edge of the mantle*) Come on now, test the odour of this mantle I have. What does it smell of? (*as Peniculus draws back*) Holding off?

Pen. The upper part of a woman's gown is the part to sniff; why, that part there taints the nose with an odour that's indetergible.

Men. (*holding out another part*) Sniff here, then, Peniculus. What dainty airs you give yourself!

Pen. So I should. (*sniffs warily*)

Men. Well now? What does it smell of? Answer.

Pen. A raid! a jade! a meal! I hope you have . . .   ***
                                                      Substitute "this mantle" for "it."
Men. Right you are! Yes, I'll take it to   (Note: "cloak" may be used throughout.)
my mistress Erotium, the courtesan here
(*pointing*) at once. I'll order luncheon to
be prepared for us immediately, for me and
you and her.

Pen. Capital!

Men. Then we'll drink and keep on drinking till the morrow's star of morn appears.

Pen. Capital! You talk to the point. (*eyeing Erotium's door anxiously*) Shall I knock now?

Men. Knock away. (*maliciously as Peniculus hurries to the door*) Or, rather, wait   Cut: "Or, rather . . . a mile." ***
a bit.

Pen. (*gloomily*) You've put the tankard back a mile.

Men. Knock gently.

Pen. I dare say you fear the door is made of Samian crockery. (*about to knock lustily when the door moves*)

Men. (*rapturously*) Wait, wait, for heaven's sake, wait! Look! she's coming out herself! Ah, you see the sun—is it not positively bedimmed in comparison with the brilliance of her body?

SCENE III

(*Enter Erotium*)

Erot. (*fondly*) My darling Menaechmus! Good day!

Pen. What about me?

Erot. (*disdainfully*) You don't count.

Pen. (*cheerfully*) A statement that applies in the army, too—it has its supernumeraries.

Men. I should like to have a (*with a nod at Peniculus*) battle prepared for me at your house there to-day.

Erot. (*puzzled, then with a smile*) To-day you shall have one.

Men. In this battle we'll both (*indicating parasite*) drink; whichever proves himself the better tankard fighter is your army: you be the judge as to—which you're to spend the night with. (*gazing at her amorously*) Oh, how I do hate my wife when I look at you, precious!

Erot. (*spying the fringe of the mantle*) Meanwhile you can't keep from wearing part of her wardrobe! (*examining it*) What is it?

Men. (*lifting his cloak*) You're arrayed and my wife's raided, rosey.

Erot. (*pleased*) Oh, of all my lovers you make me love you most, easily!

Pen. (*aside*) A courtesan is all cajolery as long as she sees something to seize upon. (*to Erotium*) Why, if you really loved him, you ought to have bitten his nose off by now.[3]

Men. (*removing his cloak*) Hold this, Peniculus; I want to make the offering I vowed.

---

[3] i.e., by kissing him passionately.

***

Precede "Knock gently." with "But."

Erotium stands, moves DSR.

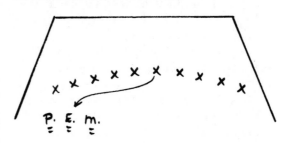

Cut: "Why, if . . . take it off, then." *****

Pen. Give it here; (*grinning at him*) but do, for heaven's sake, dance just as you are, with the mantle on, afterwards. (*takes cloak*)

Men. (*irritably*) Dance? I? Lord, man, you're crazy!

Pen. Which is more so, you or I? If you won't dance,[4] take it off, then.

Men. (*removing mantle*) It was an awful risk I ran stealing this to-day. It's my opinion Hercules never ran such a tremendous risk when he got away with the girdle of Hippolyta. (*handing it to Erotium*) Take it for your own, seeing you are the only living soul that likes to do what I like.

Erot. (*petting him*) That's the spirit that should inspire nice lovers.

Pen. (*aside, dryly*) At least such as are over-eager to plunge themselves into beggary.

Men. I bought that mantle last year for my wife, and it stood me in sixteen pounds.

Pen. (*aside*) Sixteen pounds indubitably done for, according to account rendered!

Men. Do you know what I want you to see to?

Erot. I know, I'll see to what you want.

Men. Well, then, have luncheon prepared for the three of us at your house, and have some real delicacies purchased at the forum —(*looking amused at the intent Peniculus*) savoury kernelets of pork, dried hammylets, half a pig's head, or something of the sort— things that make me hungry as a kite when served up to me well-done. And quickly, too!

Erot. Oh yes, by all means.

Men. We'll go over to the forum. Soon we'll be back here; while things are cooking we'll employ the time in drinking.

Erot. Come when you wish; we'll get ready for you.

Men. Only do hurry. (*to Peniculus, unceremoniously*) Follow me, you. (*going*)

Pen. (*at his heels*) That I will, by Jove! Watch you and follow you, both! I wouldn't take the treasures of heaven on condition of losing you this day.

(*Exeunt*)

Erot. (*going to her door and speaking to*

***

Cut speech.
Cut: "Well, then,"

He moves back to chair and sits.

He moves back to chair and sits.

---

[4] The lewd stage dancers (*cinaedi*) wore the palla.

the maids within) Call my cook Cylindrus out here at once.

Add: "I'll"

SCENE IV

(*Enter Cylindrus*)

Cylindrus stands and moves DSR.

Erot. Take a basket and some money. (*counting out some coins*) There! That's six shillings for you.

Cyl. Right, ma'am.

Erot. Go and get some provisions; see you get enough for three—neither too little nor too much.

Cyl. What sort of folks will they be?

Erot. I and Menaechmus and his parasite.

Cyl. That makes ten already, ma'am; for a parasite easily does the duty of eight men.

Erot. I have told you about the guests; attend to the rest.

Cyl. (*bustling off importantly*) Of course, ma'am. The meal is cooked; tell 'em to go in and take their places.

Erot. Come back quickly.

Cyl. I'll be here directly.

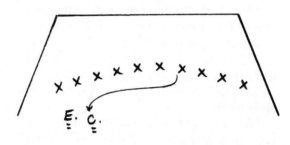

(*Exeunt*)

Erotium and Cylindrus move back to chairs and sit.

ACT II

Lights dim SR to almost blackout as lights SL come up.

SCENE I

(*Half an hour has elapsed.*)

(*Enter Menaechmus Sosicles and Messenio, followed at distance by slaves with luggage*)

Menaechmus (MS) and Messenio (Mes.) stand and move DSL.

Men. S. There is no pleasure sailors have, in my opinion, Messenio, greater than sighting from the deep the distant land.

Mes. (*sulky*) It's a greater one, to put it plainly, if the land you see, as you near the shore, was once your own. But look here, sir, why have we come now to Epidamnus? Or are we, like the sea, to go around all the islands?

Men. S. To hunt for my own twin brother.

Mes. Well, what's to be the limit to hunting for him? This is the sixth year we've been at the job. Istrians, Spaniards, Massilians, Illyrians, the entire Adriatic, and foreign Greece[5] and the whole coast of Italy—every

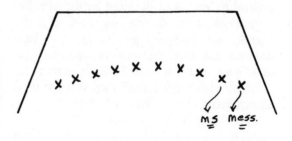

---

[5] Magna Graecia.

section the sea washes—we've visited in our travels. If you were hunting for a needle you'd have found it long ago, I do believe, if it existed. It's a dead man we keep hunting for amongst the living; why, we should have found him long ago if he were alive.

Men. S. Well then, I'm hunting for someone who can prove that to me, who can say he knows my brother is dead; I'll never take up again the task of hunting for him after that. But failing that, I'll never abandon it so long as I'm alive. I alone know how dear he is to me.

Mes. (*impatiently*) You're hunting for a knot in a bulrush. Why don't we go back home—that is, unless we're going to write a book of travels?

Men. S. (*sharply*) Do what you're told, eat what you're given, and beware of trouble. Don't annoy me—this business will not be conducted to suit you.

Mes. (*aside, peevishly*) There you are! Talk like that shows me I'm a slave. He couldn't make the case clear more concisely. But just the same I can't keep from speaking out. (*aloud*) Listen to me, sir, will you? By gad, when I inspect the wallet, our touring fund looks precious summerly. Unless you return home, by gad, I warrant you when your cash gives out while you're hunting for your twin, you'll certainly have a twinge. I tell you what, the sort of people you find here is this: In Epidamnus are the very worst of rakes and drinkers. And then the swindlers and sharpers that live in this city, no end to 'em! And then the harlot wenches —nowhere on earth are they more alluring, people say! This city got its name of Epidamnus for just this reason—because almost everyone that stops here gets damaged.

Men. S. (*dryly*) I shall look out for that. Come, hand the wallet over to me.

Mes. What do you want with it?

Men. S. I have my fears of you now, from what you say.

Mes. Fears of what?

Men. S. Of your doing me some damage in Epidamnus. You, Messenio, are a great lover of the ladies, while I am a choleric man, of ungovernable temper; so long as I hold the money I'll guard against both dan-

Cut: "He couldn't . . . speaking out." ***

***

gers—a slip on your part, and resultant choler on my own.

Mes. (*handing him the wallet, aggrieved*) Take it and keep it, do. Delighted that you should.

Scene II

(*Enter Cylindrus with provisions*)

Cyl. (*stopping and examining the contents of his basket approvingly.*) Good marketing, this, and just to my taste, too. I'll set a good lunch before the lunchers. (*looking about*) Hullo, though! There's Menaechmus! Oh, my poor back! The guests are strolling about in front of the door before I'm back with the provisions! I'll up and speak to him. (*approaches*) Good day, Menaechmus.

Men. S. (*surprised*) The Lord love you, my man, whoever you are!

Cyl. (*surprised in turn*) Whoever? Who I am?

Men. S. Gad! Indeed I don't know!

Cyl. (*deciding he jokes*) Where are the other guests?

Men. S. What guests are you looking for?

Cyl. (*grinning*) Your parasite.

Men. S. My parasite? (*to Messenio*) The fellow is certainly insane.

Mes. Didn't I tell you there was no end of swindlers here?

Men. S. What parasite of mine are you looking for, young man?

Cyl. Brush.

Mes. Brush? I've got that safe in the knapsack. Look!

Cyl. (*paying no attention to him*) You've come here to lunch too soon, Menaechmus. I'm just getting back with the provisions.

Men. S. (*gravely*) Answer me this, young man: how much do pigs cost here, sound pigs, for sacrifice?

Cyl. (*mystified*) Two shillings.

Men. S. Take two shillings from me; get yourself purified at my expense. For really it's quite clear you are insane—to bother an unknown man like me, whoever you are.

Cyl. But I'm Cylindrus. Don't you know my name?

Men. S. (*bored*) Whether you are Cylin-

Cylindrus stands, moves DSC.

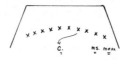

Quick glance SL.

Moves SL.

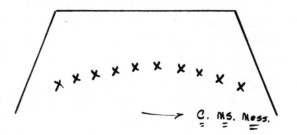

drus or Pistonus, be hanged to you! I don't know you, and more than that, I have no wish to know you.

Cyl. Your name is Menaechmus, at least as far as I know.

Men. S. You talk rationally when you call me by name. But where did you know me?

Cyl. Where did I know you, when my mistress is your sweetheart Erotium here? (*indicating house*)

Men. S. Not mine, by gad! And as for you, I don't know who you are.

Cyl. Don't know who I am, I, who serve you your wine so often when you are drinking there?

Mes. (*hotly*) Oh, blast it! Not to have a thing to smash in the fellow's head with!

Men. S. You accustomed to serve me my wine, when I never saw or set foot in Epidamnus before this day?

Cyl. You deny it?

Men. S. Gad! Indeed I do deny it!

Cyl. Don't you live in that house yonder?

Men. S. (*wrathful*) Heaven's curse light on those that do live there!

Cyl. (*aside*) He's the insane one, to be cursing his own self! (*aloud*) Listen here, Menaechmus.

Men. S. What is it?

Cyl. If you asked my advice, sir, you'd take the two shillings you recently promised me—for, by gad, it's certainly you that are lacking in sanity, to curse your own self a moment ago—and order a porker to be brought to you, if you have any sense.

Mes. Hear that! By gad, what a windy chap! He makes me tired.

Cyl. (*to audience*) He often likes to joke with me this way. He's ever so humorous— when his wife's not by. (*to Menaechmus*) I say, sir.

Men. S. Well, what do you want?

Cyl. (*pointing to basket*) Are these provisions you see enough for the three of you, or shall I get more, for you and the parasite and the lady?

Men. S. What ladies, what parasites, are you talking about, man?

Mes. What possesses you, to bother this gentleman?

Cyl. (*to Messenio, irately*) What have

you to do with me? I don't know you; I'm talking with this gentleman I do know.

Mes. Lord, man, you're not sane; I know that for sure.

Cyl. (*to Menaechmus*) Well, sir, these things shall be cooked directly, I promise you, without delay. So don't wander too far from the house. (*about to go*) Anything more I can do for you?

Men. S. Yes, go straight to the devil. (*turns away*)

Cyl. (*vehemently*) By gad, you'd better go, meanwhile, yourself—to the couch, while I (*superbly, with a wave toward the basket*) expose these things to Vulcan's violence. I'll go inside and tell Erotium you're here, so that she may bring you in rather than leave you standing here outside.

(*Exit*)   Cylindrus moves back to chair and sits.

Men. S. Gone now, has he? By Jove! I perceive those statements of yours were no lies.

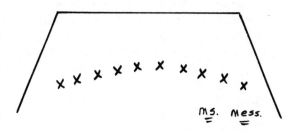

Mes. Just you keep your eyes open; for I do believe some harlot wench lives there, precisely as that madman, who just now left us, said.

Men. S. But I wonder how he knew my name?

Mes. (*with an air of vastly superior wisdom*) Lord, sir, nothing wonderful in that! This is a custom harlots have: they send their artful slaves and maids down to the port; if any foreign ship comes in, they inquire where she hails from and what her owner's name is, and then they immediately affix themselves, glue themselves fast to him. Once he's seduced, they send him home a wreck. Now in that port there (*pointing to Erotium's house*) lies a pirate bark that I surely think we'd better beware of.

Men. S. Gad, that's certainly good advice you give.

Mes. (*dissatisfied*) I'll know it's good advice when you take good care, and not before.

Men. S. (*listening*) Sh-h! Keep still a moment! The door creaked—let's see who is coming out.

Mes. (*dropping the knapsack*) Meanwhile I'll put this down. (*to the sailors, superciliously, pointing to luggage*) Kindly watch this stuff, ye ship propellers.

Cut speech.

SCENE III

(Enter Erotium into the doorway)

Erot. (*to maid within*) Leave the door so; go along, I don't want it shut. Get ready inside, look out for things, see to things, do what's necessary. (*To other maids*) Cover the couches, burn some perfumes; daintiness is what lures lovers' hearts. Attractive surroundings mean the lovers' loss and our gain. (*looking about*) But where is the man the cook said was in front of the house? Ah, yes. I see him—it's the friend I find so useful, so uncommonly helpful. And accordingly I let him quite lord it in my house as he deserves. I'll step up to him at once and give him a welcome. (*approaching Menaechmus*) Why, you darling boy, it surprises me that you should stand here outdoors when my doors are open for you and this house is more yours than your own house is. Everything is ready as you ordered and wished, and you'll meet with no delay inside. Our luncheon here has been seen to, as you ordered; you may go in and take your place when you like.

Men. S. (*to Messenio, mystified*) To whom is this woman talking?

Erot. (*surprised*) to you, of course.

Men. S. What have you had to do with me, now or ever?

Erot. (*gaily, thinking he jests*) Why, bless your heart, it has pleased Venus that I should prize you as the one man of men —and not without your deserving it. For, mercy me! you alone, with all your generosity, make me prosper.

Men. S. (*aside to Messenio*) This woman is certainly either insane or drunk, Messenio, to address a stranger like me so familiarly.

Mes. Didn't I tell you that was the way they did here? These are mere falling leaves compared with what'll happen if we stay here the next three days; then trees will fall on you. Yes, sir, harlots are like that here— they're all silver seductresses. But you just let me have a word with her. (*to Erotium, who has been looking in at her door*) Hey there, Madam! I am speaking to you.

Erot. What is it?

Mes. Where did you know this gentleman?

Erotium stands and moves DSR.

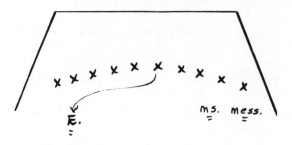

Erotium moves SL.

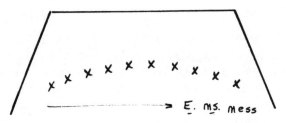

MS turns one quarter to Mes.

Erotium turns one quarter SR.
Mes. moves between Erotium and MS.

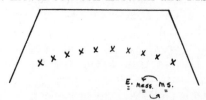

Erot. In the same place where he has long known me, in Epidamnus.

Mes. Epidamnus? When he's never set foot in this town except to-day?

Erot. Tut, tut, my smart sir! Menaechmus mine, come inside, why don't you, there's a dear. You'll find it nicer in here.

Men. S. (*aside to Messenio*) Good Lord! Now here's this woman calling me by my right name! I certainly do wonder what in the world it all means.

MS leans shoulder to shoulder into Mes.

Mes. She's scented the wallet you have.

Men. S. By Jove, yes, you have warned me wisely! Here, you take it. (*hands wallet to Messenio*) Now I'll know whether it's me or my wallet she's in love with.

Erot. (*taking his arm*) Let's go in and have luncheon.

Messenio sidesteps to the left and takes a step backward.
Erotium leans shoulder to shoulder into MS.

Men. S. (*puzzled*) Very kind of you; no, thanks.

Erot. Then why did you order me to cook luncheon for you a while ago?

Men. S. I ordered you to cook it?

Erot. Certainly, for you and your parasite.

Men. S. What parasite, confound it? (*aside to Messenio*) There's certainly something wrong with the woman's wits.

Erot. Brush, I mean.

Men. S. What brush is that? One you clean your shoes with?

Erot. Why, the one, of course, that came with you a while ago when you brought me the mantle you stole from your wife.

Men. S. What's this? I gave you a mantle I stole from my wife? Are you sane? (*to Messenio*) At any rate, this woman dreams standing up, horse fashion.

Erot. (*a little irritated*) Why is it you like to make a laughing-stock of me and deny what you did?

Men. S. Tell me what it is I did and deny.

Erot. Giving me your wife's mantle to-day.

Men. S. I deny it still. Why, I never had a wife, and have none now, and never from the day I was born have I put a foot within your city gate here. I lunched on board ship, then came ashore here, and met you.

Erot. (*aside, alarmed about him*) Look at that! Oh dear, this is dreadful! (*to Menaechmus*) What is this ship you're telling me of?

Men. S. (*flippantly*) A wooden affair, often battered about, often nailed, often pounded with a hammer; it's like a furrier's furniture, peg close to peg.

Erot. (*relieved by his jocularity and drawing him toward her door*) Now, now, do stop joking, there's a dear, and come along this way with me.

Men. S. (*releasing himself*) It is some other man you are looking for, madam, not me.

Erot. I not know you—(*playfully, as if repeating a lesson*) Menaechmus, the son of Moschus, born, so they say, in Syracuse in Sicily, where King Agathocles reigned, and after him Phintia, and thirdly Liparo, who at his death left his kingdom to Hiero, the present ruler?

Men. S. (*more perplexed*) You are quite correct, madam.

Mes. (*aside to Menaechmus*) Great Jupiter! The woman doesn't come from there, does she, to have your history so pat?

Men. S. By gad, I fancy I can't go on refusing her. (*moves toward her door*)

Mes. (*alarmed*) Don't do that! You're lost, if you cross that threshold!

Men. S. See here now, you shut up. Things are going well. I'll assent to whatever the wench says, if I can come in for entertainment here. (*confidentially to Erotium, motioning Messenio back*) I kept contradicting you a while ago purposely, my girl; I was afraid of this fellow (*indicating Messenio*)—that he might inform my wife of the mantle and the luncheon. Now when you wish let's go inside.

Erot. Shall you wait any longer for the parasite?

Men. S. Not I—I neither wait for him nor care a straw for him, nor want him admitted if he does come.

Erot. Goodness me, I'll see to that without reluctance! (*fondling him*) But do you know what I should love you to do?

Men. S. Whatever you wish—you have only to command me.

Erot. Take the mantle you gave me a while ago to the embroiderer, so as to have it repaired and have some trimmings I want added.

Men. S. Right you are, by Jove! That

will make it look different, too, and my wife won't recognize it on you, if she notices it on the street.

Erot. Well then, take it with you later when you leave me.

Men. S. By all means.

Erot. Let's go in.

Men. S. I'll follow you directly. I want another word with this fellow. (*indicating Messenio*)

(*Exit Erotium*)

Erotium moves back to chair and sits.

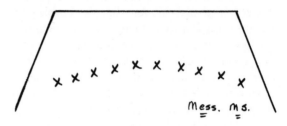

Hullo! Messenio! Step up here.

Mes. (*morose*) What's all this?

Men. S. (*elated*) Dance a jig!

Mes. What's the need of that?

Men. S. There is need. (*rather apologetic*) I know what you'll call me.

Mes. So much the worse of you.

Men. S. The booty's mine! Such siege-works as I've begun! Be off as fast as you can; take those fellows (*pointing to sailors*) to an inn at once. Then see you come to meet me before sunset.

Cut: "take. . . . then" ***
***

Mes. You don't know those harlots, master.

Men. S. Hold your tongue, I tell you. It will hurt me, not you, if I play the fool. This woman is a fool, and a silly one; from what I've observed, there's booty for us here.

(*Exit into the house*)

MS moves back to chair and sits.

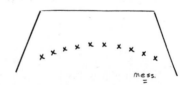

Mes. (*as if to call him back*) Oh Lord! You're gone already? Lord help him! The pirate bark is towing our yacht to perdition. But I'm a silly one to expect to manage my master; he bought me to obey his orders, not to be his commander-in-chief. (*to the sailors*) Follow me, so that I can come to meet him in season as he commanded.

Mes. moves back to chair and sits.
Cut last sentence.

(*Exeunt*)

Lights dim SL.

ACT III

SCENE I

Lights up SR.

(*Several hours have elapsed.*)

(*Enter Peniculus*)

Peniculus stands, moves DSR.

Pen. (*in high dudgeon*) More than thirty years I've lived and never in all that time have I done a worse or more accursèd deed, than to-day when I immersed myself, poor fool, in the middle of that public meeting. While I was gaping there, Menaechmus gave me the slip, and made off to his mistress, I suppose, without caring to take me along. May all the powers above consume the fellow that first devised the holding of public meetings, to busy busy men! Shouldn't they choose men with nothing to do for that sort of thing, and fine 'em forthwith if they fail to appear at the roll call? There's a plenty of men that get edibles to eat only once a day, men with no business on hand, men that are neither invited out nor invite anyone in to eat: they're the ones that ought to devote themselves to public meetings and assemblies. If this had been the rule, I shouldn't have lost my lunch to-day—for sure as I'm alive I believe he was willing to give me one. I'll join him; even now I have my sweet hopes of the leavings. (*goes towards Erotium's house as Menaechmus Sosicles comes into the doorway, wreathed and carrying the mantle*) But what do I see? Menaechmus coming out with a garland on! (*grimly*) The banquet's cleared away, and, by gad, I've come just in time to see him home! (*withdrawing*) I'll observe what the fellow's up to. Then I'll up and have a word with him.

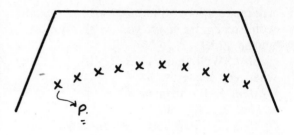

Cut: "May all . . . . me one." ***

***

MS stands, moves DSL.

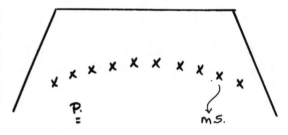

Scene II

Men. S. (*to Erotium within*) Can't you rest easy? I'll bring this back to you to-day in good season, all put in trim nicely and prettily. (*chuckling to himself*) You'll say you haven't got this one, I warrant,—it will look so unfamiliar.

Pen. (*aside, angrily*) He's carrying the mantle to the embroiderer's, now. The lunch is finished and the wine drunk, while the parasite's been shut out-of-doors! By heaven, I'm not the man I am if I don't avenge this injury and myself in beautiful style! You watch what I'll give you!

Men. S. (*leaving the doorway, jubilant*) Ye immortal gods! Did you ever in a single day bestow more blessings on any man who hoped for less? I've lunched, drunk, enjoyed

He does not carry "mantle."

the wench, and made off with this mantle, whose owner will never see it more.

Pen. (*aside*) I can't quite catch what he's talking about from this hiding-place; is it about me and the part I played, now that he's stuffed himself?

Men. S. She said I gave this to her, yes, and stole it from my wife! Seeing she was making a mistake, I at once began to agree with her, as if I had had dealings with her; whatever she said, I'd say the same. In short, I never had a good time anywhere at less expense.

Pen. (*aside his anger rising*) I'll up to the fellow! Oh, I'm aching for a row! (*steps forward*)

Men. S. (*aside*) Who's this advancing on me?

Pen. See here, you rascal lighter than a feather, you base, villainous scoundrel, you outrage of a man, you tricky good-for-nothing! What have I ever done to you that you should spoil my life? How you sneaked off from me at the forum a while ago! You've interred the luncheon, and I not there! How did you dare do it, when I was as much its heir as you?

Men. S. (*with dignity*) Sir, what have you to do with me, pray, that I, a perfect stranger, should meet with your abuse? (*dangerously*) Or do you want to be given a bad time in return for this bad language?

Pen. (*groaning*) Oh Lord! You've given me that already, I perceive, good Lord, yes!

Men. S. Pray answer me, sir, what is your name?

Pen. What? Making fun of me, as if you didn't know my name?

Men. S. Good Lord, man, I have never seen you or known you before this day, so far as I know; but—whoever you are, this much is sure—if you want to do the decent thing, don't annoy me.

Pen. Wake up, Menaechmus!

Men. S. Gad! why, I am awake, so far as I know.

Pen. You don't know me?

Men. S. I should not deny it, if I did know you.

Pen. Not know your own parasite?

Men. S. Sir, your headpiece is out of order, I perceive.

Peniculus moves SL.
After quick glance at Peniculus.

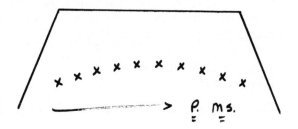

Pen. Answer me—didn't you steal that mantle from your wife to-day and give it to Erotium?

Men. S. Lord, Lord! I neither have a wife, nor gave the mantle to Erotium, nor stole it.

Pen. Really, are you sane? (*aside, in despair*) My business is done for! (*aloud*) Didn't I see you come out-doors wearing the mantle?

Men. S. Curse you! Do you think all of us follow the women, just because you do? You declare that I was wearing the mantle?

Pen. Gad, yes, of course.

Men. S. Go to—where you belong, will you! Or else get yourself purified, you utter idiot!

Pen. (*incensed*) By the Lord, no one shall ever induce me not to tell your wife everything, just as it happened! All this abuse of yours shall fall back on yourself; you shall suffer for devouring that lunch, I promise you.

Gets so incensed he closes script and backs off, getting ready to sit, speaking directly to MS.

(*Exit Peniculus into house of Menaechmus*)

He moves back to chair and sits.

Men. S. (*bewildered*) What does this mean? So everyone I set eyes on tries to make a fool of me, eh? (*listening*) But the door creaked!

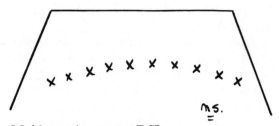

SCENE III

(*Enter Maid from Erotium's house*)

Maid stands, moves DSL.

Maid. Menaechmus, Erotium says she would very much like you to take this brace-let (*showing it*) to the jeweller's at the same time and add an ounce of gold to it and have it made over new.

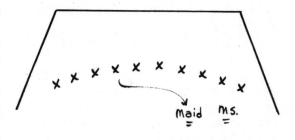

Men. S. (*taking it with alacrity*) Tell her I'll take care of that and whatever else she wants taken care of—anything she likes.

Maid. Do you know what bracelet this is?

Men. S. No, only that it's gold.

Maid. It's the one you said you stole long ago on the sly from your wife's chest.

Men. S. Good Lord, I never did!

Maid. For heaven's sake, you don't re-member? Give me back the bracelet, then, if you don't remember.

Men. S. (*thinking hard*) Wait! Yes, yes,

I do remember, to be sure! Of course, this is the one I gave her.

Maid. The very one.

Men. S. (*interestedly*) Where are those armlets I gave her along with it?

Maid. You never gave her any.

Men. S. That's right, by gad; this was all I gave her.

Maid. Shall I say you'll take care of it?

Men. S. (*hiding a smile*) Do. It shall be taken care of. I'll see she gets the bracelet back at the same time she gets the mantle.

Maid. (*coaxingly*) Menaechmus dear, do have some earrings made for me—there's a nice man!—the pendant kind, with four shillings' worth of gold in them, so that I'll be glad to see you when you visit us.

Men. S. (*heartily*) Surely. Give me the gold; I'll pay for the making, myself.

Maid. You furnish the gold, please do; I'll pay you back later.

Men. S. No, no, you give me the gold; I'll pay you back later, twice over.

Maid. I haven't it.

Men. S. Well, you give it to me when you do have it.

Maid. (*turning to go*) Is there anything else, sir?

Men. S. Say I'll take care of these things —(*aside, as maid leaves*) take care they're sold as soon as possible for what they'll bring. (*Exit Maid*) (*Looking after her*) Gone now, has she? Gone! She's shut the door. (*jubilant*) Well, well, all the gods do aid, augment, and love me! But I must hurry up and leave these harlot haunts while time and circumstance permit. Quick, Menaechmus! forward, march! I'll take off this garland and throw it away to the left (*does so*) so that if anyone follows me, they may think I have gone this way. (*going in the opposite direction*) I'll go meet my servant, if I can, and let him know how bountiful the gods have been to me.   (*Exit*)

ACT IV

SCENE I

(*Enter Menaechmus's wife from the house, followed by Peniculus*)

Wife. (*tempestuous*) Shall I let myself be

Rapidly and, again, with little regard to script.

Build in volume until Maid leaves, then long pause with coy look at audience.

Maid moves back to chair and sits.

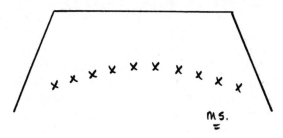

MS moves back to chair and sits.
Lights dim SL.
Lights up SR.

Wife and Pen. stand and move DSR.

made a fool of in such a married life as this, where my husband slyly sneaks off with everything in the house and carries it to his mistress?

Pen. Hush, hush, won't you? You shall catch him in the act now, I warrant you. Just you follow me this way. Drunk and garlanded, he was carrying to the embroiderer's the mantle he stole from you and carried from the house to-day. (*seeing the garland*) But look here! Here is the garland he had! Now am I a liar? There! he went this way, if you want to track him. (*looking down the street*) Yes, and by Jove, look! Splendid! He is coming back! But without the mantle!

Wife. How shall I act toward him now?

Pen. (*dryly*) The same as always—make him miserable; that is my advice. Let's step aside here; (*drawing her back between houses*) catch him from ambush.

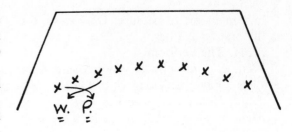

They step back and to the right.

SCENE II

(*Enter Menaechmus in a bad temper*)

Menaechmus stands, moves DSR.

Men. What slaves we are to this consummately crazy, confoundedly chafing custom! Yes, and it's the very best men amongst us that are its worst slaves. A long train of clients—that's what they all want; whether good men or bad is immaterial; it's the wealth of the clients they consider, rather than their reputation for probity. If a man's poor and not a bad sort, he's held to be an admirable client. But clients that have absolutely no regard for law, or for what is just and fair, do keep their patrons worried. They deny honest debts, are for ever at law, they're rapacious, fraudulent fellows whose money was made by usury or perjury and whose souls are centered in their lawsuits. When the day of trial is set for them, it's set for (*with increased bitterness*) their patrons, too. Up comes the case before the people, or the court, or the aedile. That's the way a certain client of mine has kept me confoundedly worried to-day, and I haven't been able to do what I wanted or have the company I wanted, he has so delayed and detained me. Before the aediles I spoke in defence of his countless atrocities,

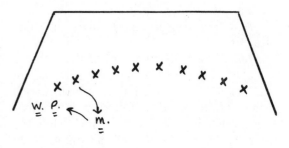

"aedile" means Roman official, police.

and proposed provisos[6] that were intricate and difficult; I had put the case more or less as was necessary to have a settlement made. But what did he do? (*hotly*) What? Named a surety! And never have I seen any man more manifestly caught; every one of his crimes was sworn to by three witnesses of the stoutest sort. (*pausing*) Heaven curse the man, with the way he's spoiled this day for me; yes, and curse me, too, for ever taking a look at the forum to-day! Such a splendid day as I have spoiled! A luncheon ordered, and a mistress no doubt waiting for me! At the earliest possible moment I hurried away from the forum. She's angry with me now, I suppose; (*hopefully*) my gift will mollify her—that mantle I took from my wife and brought to Erotium here.

Pen. (*triumphantly to wife, aside*) What do you say?

Wife. (*indignant*) That he's a wretch who has me for his wretched wife!

Pen. You quite hear what he says?

Wife. Quite.

Men. If I had any sense, I should move on and go inside where I'll have a good time. (*passes his own house and goes towards Erotium's door*)

Pen. (*stepping forward*) You wait! It will be a bad time, instead.

Peniculus and wife move down again.

Wife. (*stepping forward on the other side*) You shall certainly pay interest on that theft, I swear you shall!

Pen. (*gleefully*) Take that!

Wife. Did you think you could commit such outrages on the sly?

Men. (*guileless*) What do you mean by that, my dear?

Wife. You ask me?

Men. Do you want me to ask him? (*pointing to Peniculus*)

Peniculus stands between Men. and wife and plays one against the other.

Wife. (*as he tries to fondle her*) None of your caresses!

Pen. (*to wife*) Keep at him, keep at him!

Men. Why are you cross at me?

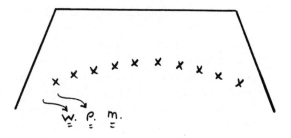

---

[6] The sponsio (*settlement*) was a kind of legal wager, each party putting up a sum of money which belonged to the party who succeeded in establishing his condicio (*proviso*). The winner of the sponsio also won the whole case. Menaechmus's client foolishly insisted upon a regular legal course and therefore praedem dedit (named a bondsman).

Wife. You ought to know!

Pen. He does know, but he's pretending, the rascal.

Men. What does this mean?

Wife. A mantle—

Men. (*worried*) A mantle?

Wife. A mantle someone—

Pen. (*to Menaechmus*) What are you frightened at?

Men. (*trying to appear unconcerned*) Frightened? I? Not in the least.

Pen. (*triumphantly, pointing to Menaechmus's face, which has turned pale*) Barring this: the mantle unmans you. Now none of your eating up the lunch behind my back! (*to Wife*) Keep at the fellow!

Men. (*aside to Peniculus*) Keep still, won't you? (*shakes his head at him.*)

Pen. (*loudly*) Indeed I will not keep still, by Jove! (*to Wife*) He's shaking his head at me not to speak.

Men. Not I, not a bit of it, by Jove! I'm not shaking my head at all, or winking at you, either.

Pen. Well, of all the cheek! To deny flatly what you see with your own eyes!

Men. My dear, I swear by Heaven and all that's holy—is that strong enough for you?—I did not shake my head at him.

Pen. Oh, she takes your word for that forthwith! Get back to the point.

Men. Back to what point?

Pen. Why, to the embroiderer's shop, I should say. Go, bring back the mantle.

Men. Mantle? What mantle?

Pen. (*disgusted at Wife's tearful futility*) I say no more, seeing she doesn't remember her own affairs.

Wife. (*in tears*) Oh Heavens! I surely am an unhappy woman!

Men. (*solicitously*) How are you unhappy? Tell me all about it. (*to Wife, tenderly*) Has any one of the slaves been at fault? Do the maids or men-servants talk back to you? Do speak out. They shall pay for it.

Wife. Nonsense!

Men. You're awfully cross. I don't quite like that.

Wife. Nonsense!

Men. It must be some one of the servants you're angry with.

Peniculus, directly to the audience.

Peniculus looks straight ahead—freeze. He can't "steal" these lines but can ruin them.

Wife. Nonsense!

Men. You're not angry at me, anyhow, are you?

Wife. There now! That's sense.

Men. Good Lord! I haven't been at fault!

Wife. Aha! back to your nonsense!   Long pause after "nonsense."

Men. (*patting her*) Do tell me what troubles you, my dear.

Pen. (*scornfully*) He's soft-soaping you, the sweet thing!

Men. (*to Peniculus*) Can't you stop annoying me? I'm not addressing you, am I? (*tries to caress his wife*)

Wife. Take your hand away! (*slaps him*)

Pen. Take that! Now be in a hurry to eat up the lunch in my absence, now get drunk and appear in front of the house with a garland on and give me the laugh!

Men. Good heavens! I haven't eaten lunch, and I've never set foot inside this house to-day.

Pen. You deny it?

Men. Indeed I do, gad, yes.

Pen. Well, of all the brazenness! Didn't I just now see you in front of the house here wearing a garland of flowers? When you told me that my headpiece was out of order and that you didn't know me, and said you were arriving from abroad?

Men. Why, I'm only this moment getting home after parting company with you a while ago.

Pen. (*angrily*) I know you! You didn't count on my having a way to get even with you. By gad, I've told your wife everything!

Men. What have you told her?

Pen. Oh, I don't know; ask her yourself.

Men. (*to his wife, bravely*) What's all this, my dear? What sort of a tale has he been relating to you? What is it? Why are you silent? Why don't you tell me what it is?

Wife. As if you didn't know! Asking me!

Men. Bless my soul! I shouldn't ask you if I did know.

Pen. Oh the villain! How he plays the innocent! (*to Menaechmus*) You can't conceal it; she understands the matter beautifully. I have told her the whole story, by Jove!

Men. What does this mean?

Wife. (*with acerbity*) Since you have no

sense of shame and no wish to confess of
your own free will, listen, and listen closely.
I'll soon let you know why I'm cross and
what he told me. A mantle has been stolen
from me at home.

Men. (*indignant*) A mantle stolen from
me?

Pen. See how the rascal is trying to catch
you? (*to Menaechmus*) It was stolen from
her, not from you. Why, if it was stolen from
you, it would certainly be—lost.[7]

Men. (*to Peniculus*) I have nothing to
do with you. (*to Wife*) But you, what are
you saying?

Wife. A mantle, I tell you, has disap-
peared from the house.

Men. Who stole it?

Wife. Goodness me! The man who took
it knows that.

Men. Who is this man?

Wife. A certain Menaechmus.

Men. It's a scurvy trick, by Jove! Who is
this Menaechmus?

Wife. You yourself, I tell you.

Men. I?

Wife. You.

Men. Who's my accuser?

Wife. I am.

Pen. Yes, and I. And you took it to your
mistress Erotium here, too.

Men. I gave it away—I?

Wife. You, you yourself, I tell you.

Pen. D'ye want us to bring on an owl, to
keep saying "yoo, yoo" to you? For we've
got tired of saying it by now.[8]

Men. (*weakly*) But I didn't give it to her
out and out; I only—it's like this—I only
lent it.

Wife. Good gracious, sir! I certainly do
not lend out your mantle or cloak to anyone.
A woman is the proper person to give out
women's clothes, a man men's. You bring
that mantle back home, will you?

Men. I'll see it's brought back.

Wife. You will be seeing to your own
comfort, I fancy; for never shall you enter
the house unless you bring the mantle with

---

[7] and not safe at the embroiderer's.
[8] vv. 655–656: *Men.* My dear, I swear by Heaven
and all that's holy—is that strong enough for you?
—I did not give it away.
Wife. Goodness me, no, that we are not lying.

you. (*turning away abruptly*) I am going home.

Pen. (*anxiously*) What do I get for helping you in this?

Wife. (*with a sour smile*) I'll help you in return when something is stolen from your house.

(Exit into the house)

Pen. Oh Lord! That means never, for I have nothing in my house to lose. (*heartily*) Be damned to you, husband and wife both! I'll hurry to the forum, for I perceive I've plainly fallen out of the good graces of this family. (*Exit*)

Men. (*comfortably*) My wife thinks she has pained me by shutting me out. Just as if there wasn't another place—and a better one—where I'll be admitted. If you don't like me, I must bear it; Erotium here will like me anyway. She won't shut me out; oh no, she'll shut me in with her! Now I'll go and beg her to give me back the mantle I gave her a while ago; I'll buy her another, a better one. (*knocking at the door*) Hullo! Anyone minding the door here? Open up and call Erotium out, someone!

SCENE III

Erot. (*within*) Who is inquiring for me?

Men. A man who is more his own foe than yours, dear.

(Enter Erotium into the doorway)

Erot. Menaechmus, love, why are you standing out here? (*taking his arm*) Do come in.

Men. Wait. Do you know why I've come to see you?

Erot. I know—so that we may have a nice time together.

Men. No, you're wrong, confound it! Do give me back that mantle I gave you a while ago, there's a dear. My wife has found out about the whole business, from beginning to end. I'll buy you a mantle twice as expensive—any you choose.

Erot. (*surprised*) But I gave it to you to take to the embroiderer's just a few minutes ago, along with that bracelet you were to carry to the jeweller's to have made over.

Wife moves back to chair and sits.

Peniculus moves back to chair and sits.

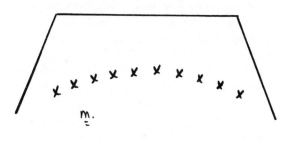

Erotium stands and delivers line, then she

moves DSR.

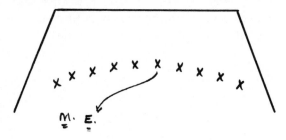

Men. You gave me the mantle and a bracelet—me? You'll find you never did so. Why, after giving you that mantle a while ago and going to the forum, I'm just getting back; this is the first time I've seen you since then.

Erot. (*aroused*) But I see what you are up to. Just because I've put them into your hands you're attempting to do this, to cheat me.

Men. No, heavens, no! it's not to cheat you I ask for it—really, my wife has found out, I tell you—

Erot. (*passing over what she thinks the usual lie*) No, and I didn't beg you to give it to me in the first place; you brought it to me yourself of your own accord, made me a present of it; and now you ask it back. Very well. Take it, carry it off, wear it yourself or let your wife wear it, or for that matter lock it up in a coffer. You shall not set foot in the house after to-day, don't fool yourself. Now that you've held a good friend like me in contempt, you can bring along ready money, or else you can't lead me along like a fool. After this you just find somebody else to fool. (*turns to go in*)

Men. Oh gad, now, really you're too testy! Here, here! I say! Wait! Come back! What? you won't stop? What? you aren't willing to return for my sake?

(*Exit Erotium, slamming the door*)

She's gone inside! She's closed the door! Well, if I'm not getting the most exclusive reception! Neither at home nor at my mistress's either, do they believe a word I say! I'll go and consult my friends about this and see what they think should be done.

(*Exit*)

She turns quickly, walking swiftly to her chair and sits.

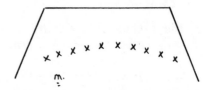

He moves back to his chair and sits.

ACT V

SCENE I

(*Enter Menaechmus Sosicles*)

Men. S. What an idiot I was a while ago when I entrusted my wallet and money to Messenio! He's immersed himself in a pothouse somewhere, I suppose.

Lights change from SR to SL.

MS stands and moves DSL.

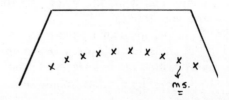

(Enter the Wife of Menaechmus into the doorway)

Wife. I'll go out and see if my husband won't soon be back home. (*Seeing Menaechmus Sosicles*) Oh, why, there he is! I'm saved! He is bringing back the mantle.

Men. S. I wonder where Messenio is promenading now.

Wife. I'll step up and welcome him with the words he deserves. (*advancing*) Aren't you ashamed to appear in my sight with that costume, you monster?

Men. S. (*startled*) Eh, what is it that excites you, madam?

Wife. What! Do you dare breathe a word, do you dare speak to me, you shameless creature?

Men. S. What, pray, is my offence, that I should not dare to speak?

Wife. You ask me? Oh, such brazen shamelessness!

Men. S. (*still polite*) Madam, do you not know why the ancient Greeks used to declare that Hecuba was a bitch?

Wife. (*sharply*) No, indeed I don't.

Men. S. Because Hecuba used to do precisely what you are doing now: she used to pour every kind of abuse on everyone she saw. So they began to call her bitch, and quite properly, too.

Wife. (*incensed*) I cannot endure this outrageous conduct of yours. Why, I'd rather live without a husband all my life than put up with the outrageous things you do.

Men. S. And how does it concern me whether you can endure your married life, or leave your husband? Or is this the fashion here—to prattle to arriving strangers?

Wife. Prattle? I will not put up with it any longer, I tell you. I'll get a divorce rather than tolerate your goings-on.

Men. S. Lord, Lord! get divorced, for all I care—and stay so as long as Jove reigns!

Wife. (*examining mantle*) See here, you denied stealing this a while ago, and now you hold it, the very same one, right before my eyes. Aren't you ashamed?

Men. S. Bravo, madam! By Jove! You are a bold, bad one with a vengeance! Do you dare tell me this was stolen from you, when another woman gave it to me so that I might get it renovated?

Wife stands and delivers first line, then moves DSL during next speech.

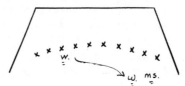

Moves DSL.

Wife. Good heavens, this is—I'll send for my father this moment and I'll give him an account of your outrageous actions! (*calling at door*) Deceo! Go look for my father—bring him here to me; say it's absolutely necessary. (*to Menaechmus Sosicles*) I'll soon lay bare your outrageous conduct!

Men. S. Are you sane? What is this outrageous conduct of mine?

Wife. You filched my mantle and jewellery from the house—from your own wife—and carried them off to your mistress. Isn't this perfectly true (*bitterly*) prattle?

Men. S. Good Lord, madam, if you know of any drug I can take to enable me to endure that temper of yours, for heaven's sake name it. Who you think I am is a mystery to me; as for me, I knew you when I knew Hercules' wife's grandfather.[9]

Wife. You may laugh at me, but I vow you can't laugh at that man (*pointing down the street*), my father, who's coming this way. Look back there. Do you know him?

Men. S. (*looking*) Oh yes, I knew him when I knew Calchas.[10] I saw him on the same day I first saw you.

Wife. You deny knowing me, you deny knowing my father?

Men. S. Oh, Lord! I'll say the same thing if you bring on your grandfather. (*walks away*)

Wife. Oh dear me! that's just the way you are always acting!

Scene II

(*Enter Menaechmus' Father-in-law slowly and laboriously.*)

Father (*sighing wearily*) Yes, I'll step out, I'll step along as . . . fast as my age permits and the occasion demands.(*halting*) But I know well enough how . . . easy it is for me. For I've lost my nimbleness . . . the years have taken hold of me . . . it's a heavy body I carry . . . my strength has left me. Ah, old age is a bad thing—a bad piece of freight! Yes, yes, it brings along untold tribulations when it comes; if I were to specify them all, it would be a . . . long,

---

[9] Porthaon, father of Oeneus, father of Deianeira, last wife of Hercules.

[10] a seer at the siege of Troy.

Father-in-law stands, moves DSR.

MS and Wife look out into space and occasionally reflect enjoyment of the Father-in-law's speech. (Do NOT follow script on his speech.)

long story. But this is the thing that weighs on my mind and heart—what in the world has happened to make my daughter ask me, all of a sudden this way, to come to her. Not a word am I told as to what is wrong, what she wants, why she summons me. However, I have a pretty fair notion already what it's all about. She's had some squabble with her husband, I fancy. That's the way with women that try to keep their husbands under their thumbs, arrogant just because they've brought a good dowry. (*pauses*) And the husbands often aren't blameless, either. (*reflecting*) However, there's a limit, just the same, to what a wife should put up with; and by Jove, a daughter never summons her father unless there's something amiss or some just cause for complaint. But I shall soon know about it, whatever it is. (*advancing and looking about*) Ah, there she is herself in front of the house—and her husband, looking sour! It's just as I suspected. I'll have a word with her.

Wife. (*aside*) I'll go meet him. (*advancing*) I hope you're well, father dear—very well.

She moves across to SR.

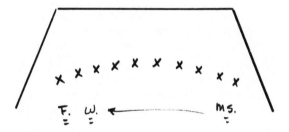

Father. And you. Do I find all well here? Is all well, that you have me summoned? Why are you so gloomy? Yes, and why is he (*pointing to Menaechmus Sosicles*) standing aloof there, angry? You've been bickering over something or other, you two. Out with it—which is to blame? Be brief; no long words.

Wife. I haven't been at fault at all, indeed I haven't; I'll relieve you on this point first, father. But I can't live here, I simply cannot stand it. So you must take me away from this house.

Father. (*peevishly*) But what is the trouble?

Wife. I'm made a laughing-stock, father!

Father. By whom?

Wife. By the man you entrusted me to, my husband.

Father. Now look at that! A squabble! See here, how many times have I given you notice to guard against coming to me with grievances, either of you?

Wife. (*tearfully*) How can I guard against that, father dear?

Father. (*severely*) You ask me?

Wife. If you please.

Father. How many times have I explicitly told you to humour your husband and not keep watching what he does, where he goes, and what he is about?

Wife. Well, but he makes love to this strumpet, the very next door!

Father. He shows excellent judgment, and he will make love to her all the more, I warrant you, to reward this diligence of yours.

Wife. And he drinks there, too.

Father. Just because of you, will he drink the less there or anywhere else he pleases? Such confounded impudence! You might as well expect to keep him from accepting an invitation to dinner, or from having company at his own home. Do you expect your husband to be your slaves? You might as well expect to give him housework to do, and bid him sit with the maids and card wool.

Wife. (*resentfully*) I see I have brought you here, father, to defend my husband, not myself. Retained by me, you plead his case.

Father. If he has done anything out of the way, I shall be a great deal more severe with him than I have been with you. But inasmuch as he keeps you well supplied with jewellery and clothes, furnishes you with plenty of maidservants and provisions, you had better be sensible about things, my girl.

Wife. But he filches my jewellery and mantles from my chests at home, he robs me, and carries my nicest things to strumpets on the sly!

Father. He does wrong, if he does that; if he doesn't, you are doing wrong to accuse an innocent man.

Wife. Why, he has a mantle this very moment, father, and a bracelet he'd taken to her he is just now bringing back, because I found him out.

Father. I'll find out about this from him at once. I'll go and have a talk with the man. (*approaching Menaechmus Sosicles*) Speak up, Menaechmus, and let me know what you two are at odds over. Why are you so gloomy? And why is she standing aloof there, angry?

Men. S. (*vehemently*) Whoever you are,

Father-in-law moves SL.

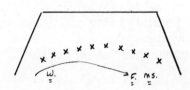

whatever your name is, old gentleman, I call Heaven and God on high to witness—

Father. (surprised) What about, concerning what conceivable thing?

Men. S. That I have done no wrong to that woman who accuses me of having raided her house and stolen this mantle, and of having carried it off—

Wife. He swears to that?

Men. S. If I ever set foot inside this house, where she lives, I pray Heaven to make me the most wretched wretch on earth.

Father. (horrified) Are you sane, to pray for a thing like that, or to deny that you ever put foot in this house, where you live, you utter idiot?

Men. S. Do you, too, say I live in that house, old gentleman?

Father. And do you deny it?

Men. S. By gad I do, truly!

Father. No, by gad, you do untruly— unless you moved away somewhere last night. *(turning to his wife)* Daughter, come over here. *(she obeys)* Tell me—you have not moved away from here, have you?

Cut: "Daughter, come over here."

Wife. Where to, or why, for mercy's sake?

Father. Bless my soul, I don't know.

Wife. He's making fun of you, of course. Can't you see that?

Father. Really now, Menaechmus, you have joked enough. Come now, stick to the point!

Men. S. See here, what have I got to do with you? Who are you, and where do you come from? What do I owe you, or that woman either, who is pestering me in every conceivable way?

Wife. (to her father, frightened) Do you see how green his eyes are? And that greenish colour coming over his temples and forehead? How his eyes glitter! look!

Men. S. (aside) Seeing they declare I'm insane, what's better for me than to pretend I am insane, so as to frighten them off? *(develops alarming symptoms)*

Wife. (more frightened) How he stretches and gapes! Father, father dear, what shall I do now?

Father (retreating) Come over here, my child, as far as you can from him!

Cut speech. Father-in-law moves SR.

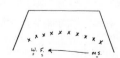

Men. S. (having worked himself up properly) Euhoe! Bacchus! Bromius! Whither dost thou summon me a-hunting in the

woods? I hear, but I cannot quit these re-
gions, with that rabid bitch on watch there
at my left, aye, and there behind a bald-
headed goat who many a time in his life has
ruined a guiltless fellow-citizen by his perjury!

Father. (*in helpless rage*) Ugh! Curse
you!

Men. S. Lo! Apollo from his oracle doth
bid me burn her eyes out with blazing
brands!

Wife. He'll murder me, father dear! he
threatens to burn my eyes out!

Father. (*in low tone*) Hey! daughter!

Wife. What is it? What shall we do?

Father. How about my calling the servants
here? I'll go and fetch some to carry him
away from here and tie him up at home before he makes any more trouble.

Men. S. (*aside*) Now then, I'm stuck!
Unless I get the start of them with some
scheme, they'll be taking me off to their
house. (*intercepting the old man and glaring at Wife*) Thou dost bid me, Apollo, to
spare my fists in no wise upon her face, unless she doth leave my sight and—get to
the devil out of here! I will do as thou biddest, Apollo! (*advancing upon her*)

Father. Run, run home as fast as you can
before he batters you to bits!

Wife. (*rushing for the door*) Yes, I'm
running. Do, please, keep watch of him,
father dear, and don't let him leave this
place! Oh, miserable woman that I am, to
have to hear such words!   (*Exit*)

Men S. Not badly, oh Apollo, did I remove that female! Now for this beastly,
bewhiskered, doddering Tithonus, who calls
himself the son of Cygnus[11]—these be thy
commands, that I crush his limbs and bones
and joints with that same staff which he doth
carry! (*advances*)

Father. (*retreating and raising his staff*)
You'll get hurt if you touch me, I tell you,
or if you come any nearer to me!

Men. S. I will do as thou biddest! I will
take a double-edged axe, and this old man—
I'll hew away his flesh, gobbet by gobbet, to
the very bone!

---

[11] A mistake, probably intentional. Tithonus was the
son of Laomedon.

Wife moves back to chair and sits.

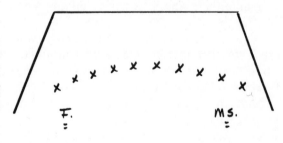

Father. (*aside, timorously, still retreating*) I must be on my guard and look out for myself, indeed I must! Really, I'm afraid he'll do me some injury, from the way he threatens me.

Men. S. Many are thy commands, Apollo. Now thou dost bid me take yokéd steed, unbroken, fiery, and mount a chariot that I may bash to earth this aged, stinking, toothless lion. (*mounts his chariot*) Now am I in my car! Now do I hold the reins! Now have I goad in hand! On, steeds, on! Let the ring of your hoof-beats be heard! Let your fleetness of foot rush you rapidly on! (*gallops about*)

He does not "gallop!"
There is no "staff."

Father. (*clutching his staff*) You threaten me with yokéd steeds—me?

Men. S. Lo, Apollo! Anew thou biddest me charge upon this man who stands here and lay him low! (*Charges; the old man raises his staff; the charioteer stops short*) But who is this who by the hair doth tear me from the car? He revokes thy command and the edict of Apollo! (*falls to the ground, apparently senseless*)

He does not fall.

Father. Well! Good heavens, what an acute, severe attack! Lord save us! Now this man who's gone insane—how healthy he was a little while ago! For him to have such an attack so suddenly! I'll go and summon a doctor as soon as I possibly can.   (*Exit*)

Father-in-law moves back to chair and sits.

Scene III

Men. S. (*getting up and looking about*) For Heaven's sake, are they out of my sight now, those two that absolutely compelled me, sound though I am, to go insane? I'd better hurry off to the ship while I can do so safely. (*to audience*) I beg you, all of you, if the old man comes back, don't tell him which way I bolted.   (*Exit*)

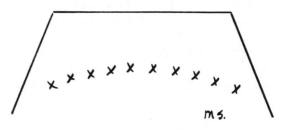

MS moves back to chair and sits.

(*Enter Father-in-law*)

Father. My loins ache from sitting and my eyes from watching, while I waited for the doctor to come back from his calls. Finally he did manage to get away from his patients, the bore! He says he set a broken leg for Aesculapius, and put Apollo's arm in a splint, besides! So now I am wondering whether to say I'm bringing a sawbones or

Cut speech.

a stonecutter. (*glancing down the street*) Just look at him mince along! (*calling*) Quicken that ant's pace of yours!

SCENE IV

(*Enter a Doctor*)

Doctor. (*ponderously*) What was the nature of his attack, did you say? State the symptoms, old gentleman. Is it a demoniacal visitation or paranoia? Inform me. Does he suffer from a lethargical habit or intercutaneous fluid?

Father. (*sharply*) Why, I brought you just to tell me that and cure him.

Doctor. (*lightly*) Oh, that is easy, quite easy. He shall be cured—I promise you that upon my honour.

Father. (*distrustfully*) I want him to be cared for very carefully indeed.

Doctor. (*reassuringly waggish*) Why, I will sigh more than six hundred times a day; that shows how I will care for him very carefully indeed for you.

Father. (*looking down street*) Ah, there is our man himself! Let's watch what he does. (*they step back*)

Father-in-law and Doctor move DSL.

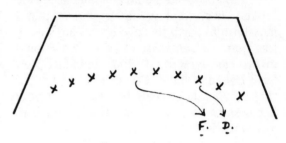

SCENE V

(*Enter Menaechmus*)

Men. Good Lord! This was certainly proved a perverse and adverse day for me! Everything I thought I was doing on the sly has got out, thanks to that parasite who's over-whelmed me with infamy and fear— that Ulysses of mine who's brewed such a mess for his lord and master! Sure as I'm alive, I'll shuffle off that fellow's mortal coil! His? I'm a fool to call it his, when it's mine; it's my food and my money he's been reared on. I'll cut that worthy off from the breath of life! But as for the harlot, she was true to style, did only what her class always do! Because I ask her to let me carry the mantle back to my wife again, she says she has given it to me. Well! By Jove, I certainly do lead a miserable life!

Father. (*to Doctor*) Do you catch what he says?

Doctor. He declares that he is miserable.

Father. I should like you to go up to him.

Menaechmus stands, moves DSR.

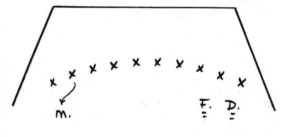

Doctor. (*advancing*) Good day, Menaechmus. But, my dear man, why do you expose your arm? Are you not aware how injurious that is to one suffering from your present complaint?

Men. (*violently*) You be hanged! (*the Doctor jumps*)

Father. (*aside to Doctor*) Do you notice anything?

Doctor. I should say I do. This case is beyond the powers of a wagonload of hellebore. But see here, Menaechmus.

Men. What d'ye want?

Doctor. Answer me this question: do you drink white or red wine?

Men. Oh, go to the devil!

Doctor. (*to Father*) Ah yes, now he begins to manifest the first symptoms of insanity.

Men. Why don't you inquire whether the bread I generally eat is blood red, rose red, or saffron yellow? Whether I generally eat birds with scales, fish with feathers?

Father. (*to Doctor*) Dear, dear! Do you hear how wildly he talks? Why don't you hurry up and give him a dose of something before he goes insane entirely?

Doctor. (*to Father*) Now, now, one moment! I will question him still further.

Father. You're killing me with your talk!

Doctor. (*to patient*) Tell me this: do you ever experience a sensation of hardness in the eyes?

Men. What? You good-for-nothing, do you take me for a lobster?

Doctor. Tell me: do you ever have a rumbling of the bowels, so far as you observe?

Men. Not after I've had a square meal; when I'm hungry, then there's a rumbling.

Doctor. (*to Father*) Well, well! There's no indication of insanity in that reply. (*to Menaechmus*) Do you sleep entirely through the night? Do you fall asleep readily on retiring?

Men. I sleep through if I've paid my bills —(*angrily*) may all the powers above consume you, you inquisitive ass!

Doctor. (*backing away*) Now the man does begin to manifest insanity! You hear him—look out for yourself!

Father. Oh no, to hear him now you'd

Doctor moves SR.
Cut: "But . . . complaint." ***

***

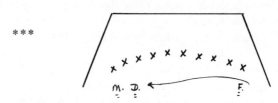

Cut: "This case . . . But" ***

***

Father-in-law moves SR.

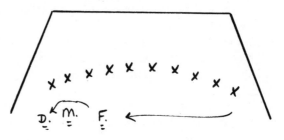

think him a perfect Nestor[12] compared with what he was a while ago. Why, a while ago he called his wife a rabid bitch.

Men. Eh? I?

Father. Yes, while you were raving.

Men. I?

Father. Yes, you, and you kept threatening me, too—that you would dash me to the earth with a yokéd four-in-hand. I myself saw you do all this. I myself accuse you of it.

Men. (*incensed*) Yes, and you stole the sacred crown from Jupiter's statue, I know that; and you were put in prison for it, I know that; and after getting out, you were put in the stocks and whipped, I know that; and then you murdered your father and sold your mother, that's something more I know. Do I pay you back your abuse well enough for a sane man, eh?

Father. For God's sake, doctor, whatever you're going to do, hurry up and do it! Don't you see the man is insane?

Doctor. (*aside to Father*) Do you know what you had best do? Have him conveyed to my house.

Father. You advise that?

Doctor. By all means. There I shall be able to care for him as I deem expedient.

Father. Do as you please.

Doctor. (*to Menaechmus*) You shall drink Hellebore, I promise you, for some twenty days.

Men. But I'll string you up and jab goads into you for thirty days.

Doctor. (*aside to Father*) Go, summon men to convey him to my house.

Father. How many are needed?

Doctor. Considering the degree of insanity I note, four, no less.

Father. They shall be here soon. Keep watch of him, doctor.

Doctor. (*clearly reluctant*) No, no! I shall go home so as to make the necessary preparations. You order the servants to bring him to my house.

Father. He'll be there soon, I promise you.

Doctor. I am going.

Father. Good-bye.   (*Exeunt*)

Doctor and Father-in-law move back to chairs and sit.

---

[12] the counsellor of the Greeks at Troy.

Men. (*looking after them*) Father-in-law's gone. Doctor's gone. All alone! Lord save us! What is it makes those men declare I'm insane? Why, as a matter of fact, I've never had a sick day since I was born. I'm neither insane, nor looking for fights, nor starting disputes, not I. I'm perfectly sound and regard others as sound; I recognize people, talk to them. Can it be they're insane themselves with their absurd statements that I'm insane? (*pauses*) What shall I do now? I long to go home, but my wife won't let me. And as for this place, (*glaring at Erotium's house*) no one will let me in. Oh what damnable luck! (*pauses*) Here's where I'll stay, indefinitely; I fancy I'll be let into the house at nightfall, anyhow.

Scene VI

(*Enter Messenio*)

Mes. (*self-righteous and smug*) This is your proof of a good servant who looks after his master's business, sees to it, gives it his care and consideration—when he watches over his master's business in his master's absence just as diligently as if he was present, or even more so. The chap that's got his wits in the proper place ought to think more of his back than his gullet, more of his shanks than his belly. He'd better recollect how good-for-nothings, lazy, rascally fellows are rewarded by their masters: whippings, shackles, work in the mill, fag, famine, freezing stiff—these are the rewards of laziness. I'm badly afraid of such bad things, personally; that's why I've made up my mind to lead a good life rather than a bad one. I can stand chiding a great deal more easily—but a hiding I can't abide, myself, and I'd very much rather eat the meal than turn the mill. That's why I follow out master's orders, attend to 'em properly and sedately; yes, indeed, I find it pays. Others can act as they think good for 'em; I'm going to be the sort of chap I should be—I must have a sense of fear, I must keep straight, so as to be on hand for master anywhere.[13] I shan't have much to fear. The

[13] vv. 983A–983B: Servants that are afraid even when they're blameless, they're the ones that are always of some use to their masters. And I tell you, the ones that aren't afraid at all are afraid all right after they've earned a thrashing.

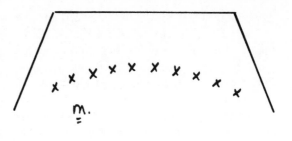

Menaechmus moves back to chair and sits.

Messenio stands, moves DSL.

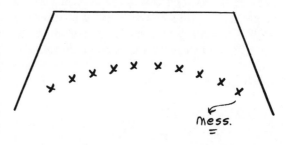

"fag" means to labor to weariness.

day's near when master will reward me for my service. I do my work on the principle that I think is good for my back. Here I come to meet master just as he told me, now that I've left the luggage and slaves at an inn. Now I'll knock at the door, so as to let him know I'm here, and lead him safely out of this ravine of ruination. But I'm afraid I'll be too late and find the battle over. (*goes to Erotium's doorway*)

SCENE VII

(*Enter Father-in-law with Slaves*)

Father. (*to Slaves, sternly*) By heaven and earth, I charge you to be wise and heed my orders, past and present. Pick up that man (*indicating Menaechmus*) and carry him at once to the doctor's office—that is, unless you have no regard at all for your legs or flanks. See that none of you cares a straw for his threats. Why are you standing still? Why are you hesitating? He ought to have been hoisted up and carried off already. I'll go to the doctor's; I'll be at hand there when you arrive. (*Exit*)

Men. (*as the Slaves dash at him*) Murder! What does this mean? What are those fellows rushing at me for, in the name of Heaven? What do you want? What are you after? What are you surrounding me for? Where are you pulling me? Where are you carrying me? (*struggling on their shoulders*) Murder! Help, help, Epidamnians, I beg you! Save me, fellow citizens! Let me go, I tell you!

Mes. Ye immortal gods! In Heaven's name, what is this my eyes behold? My master being carried off by some gang of rowdies in most outrageous fashion!

Men. Doesn't anyone dare come to my rescue?

Mes. (*running up*) I do, master,—like a regular daredevil! (*yelling lustily*) Oh, what an outrage, what a shame, Epidamnians! My master, a free-born visitor amongst you, to be abducted here in time of peace, in broad daylight, in your city streets! Let go of him!

Men. For Heaven's sake, whoever you are,

Messenio moves back to his chair and sits.

Menaechmus stands, moves DSR.
Father-in-law stands, moves DSL.

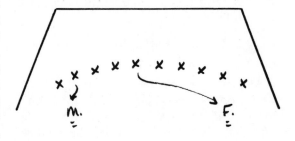

Father-in-law moves back to his chair and sits.

Messenio stands, moves SL.

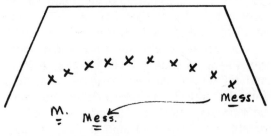

Messenio arriving SL.

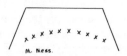

This fight with the slaves must be boisterous reading built to help your audience simulate a knock-down, drag-out battle.

stand by me and don't let me be maltreated in such atrocious fashion!

Mes. Not I! Stand by you I will, and defend you and help you with all my heart! I won't let you be murdered, never! Better myself than you! For Heaven's sake, master, pull out the eye of that chap that has you by the shoulder! (*swinging vigorously at the nearest Slave*) As for these fellows here, I'm going to seed down their faces for them directly and plant my fists. By gad, you'll pay dear this day for carrying him off! Let go!

Men. I've got this one by the eye!

Mes. Leave the socket showing in his head! (*warming up to his work*) You rascals! You robbers! You bandits!

Slaves. Murder! Oh, for God's sake, let up!

Cut speech.

Mes. Let go, then! (*they drop Menaechmus*)

Men. (*assisting Messenio*) What do you mean by touching me? (*to Messenio*) Comb them down with your fists! (*Slaves scatter*)

Mes. Come, clear out! Get to the devil out of here! (*with a parting kick to a laggard*) There's another for you—take as a prize for being the last to leave!

(*Exeunt Slaves*)

Long pause.

(*Smirking*) Oh, I measured their faces in fine style and quite to my taste. By Jove, master, I certainly did come to your aid in the nick of time just now!

Men. Well, Heaven bless you for ever and ever, young man, whoever you are. For if it hadn't been for you, I should never have lived to see the sun go down this day.

Mes. Then, by Jove, master, if you did the right thing you'd set me free.

Men. I set you free?

Mes. Yes indeed, seeing I saved your life, master.

Men. What's this? You're making a mistake, young man.

Mes. Eh? A mistake?

Men. Why, I swear by Father Jupiter I'm not your master.

Mes. (*protestingly*) Oh, none of that, sir!

Men. I'm not lying; no slave of mine ever did such a thing as you did for me.

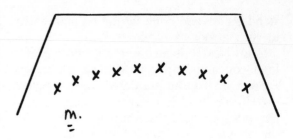

Mes. Very well then, sir, if you say I'm not yours, let me go free.

Men. Lord, man, be free so far as I am concerned, and go where you like.

Mes. (*eagerly*) Those are your orders, really?

Men. Lord, yes, if I have any authority over you.

Mes. (*wild with joy*) Hail, patron mine! "Messenio, I congratulate you on your freedom!" By gad, I take your word for it! But, patron, I beseech you, don't order me about any less than when I was your slave. I intend to live with you, and when you go home I'll go with you.

Men. (*aside*) Oh no you won't.

Mes. Now I'll go to the inn and fetch the luggage and cash for you. The wallet with the travelling money is duly under seal in the bag; I'll bring it here to you directly.

Men. (*interested*) Be quick about it.

Mes. I'll give it back to you intact, sir, just as you gave it to me. Wait for me here.

(*Exit*)

Messenio moves back to chair and sits.

Men. Well, well, how strangely strange things have happened to me today! Here are people saying I'm not myself and shutting me out of doors, and there's that fellow who just now said he was going to fetch me some money and that he was my slave—that saviour of mine, whom I just now set free. He says he'll bring me a wallet with money in it; if he does, I'll tell him to leave me and enjoy his freedom wherever he likes, so that he won't be coming to me for his money when he regains his sanity. (*pauses*) My father-in-law and the doctor said I was insane. It's a marvel to me what all this means! It seems just like a dream. (*reflects*) Now I will go into this harlot's house, no matter if she is in a rage with me, and see if I can't induce her to give me back the mantle to carry back home.

Menaechmus moves back to his chair and sits.

(*Exit into Erotium's house*)

SCENE VIII

(*Enter Menaechmus Sosicles
and Messenio*)

MS and Messenio stand and move DSL.

Men. S. You cheeky rascal, you have the

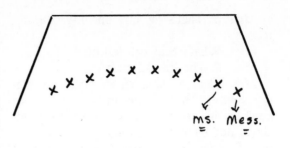

cheek to tell me you have encountered me anywhere to-day since the time I ordered you to come here and meet me?

Mes. (*much aggrieved*) Why, sir, I just now rescued you when four men were carrying you off on their shoulders in front of this very house. You were yelling for all heaven and earth to help you, when up I ran and rescued you by good hard fighting, in spite of 'em. And for this, because I'd saved you, you've set me free. Then the moment I said I was going to get the money and luggage, you ran ahead as fast as you could to meet me, so as to deny what you had done!

Men. S. So I ordered you to go free, eh?

Mes. (*hopefully*) Certainly, sir.

Men. S. (*emphatically*) Well, the most certain thing in the world is this—I had rather become a slave myself than ever free you.

SCENE IX

(*Enter Menaechmus from Erotium's house*)

Menaechmus stands, moves DSR.

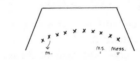

Men. (*to those within*) Swear it by the eyes in your head if you like, but, by the Lord, that won't make it any more true that I took off the mantle and bracelet to-day, you sluts!

Cut "you sluts."

Mes. (*gazing at him*) Ye immortal gods, what do I see?

Men. S. What do you see?

Mes. Your mirror!

Men. S. What do you mean?

Mes. (*pointing to Menaechmus*) He's the very image of you! He's as like you as can be!

Men. S. (*comparing himself with the stranger*) By Jove! He certainly is not unlike me, now that I look myself over.

Men. (*seeing Messenio*) Ah there, sir, bless you—you that saved me, whoever you are!

Mes. Sir, for the love of Heaven, do tell me your name, if you don't object.

Men. Gad, man, your services to me haven't been such that I should grudge meeting your wishes. My name is Menaechmus.

Men. S. (*startled*) Good Lord, no; it's mine!

Men. I'm a Sicilian—a Syracusan.

Men. S. That's my city and my country, too.

Men. What's that you tell me?

Men. S. The simple truth.

Mes. (*half to himself, as he scans Menaechmus*) This is the man I know, of course; this is my master. I'm really his slave, but I fancied (*glancing at Menaechmus Sosicles*) I was his. (*to Menaechmus*) I thought he was you, sir, and what's more, I made myself a nuisance to him, too. (*to Menaechmus Sosicles*) I beg your pardon, sir, if I said anything silly to you without realising it.

Men. S. (*sharply*) You talk like an idiot. Do you not remember coming ashore along with me to-day?

Mes. (*hurriedly*) To be sure, you're right. It's you who are my master. (*to Menaechmus*) You seek another slave. (*to Menaechmus Sosicles*) Good day to you, sir. (*to Menaechmus*) Good-bye to you, sir. I say this gentleman (*indicating his master*) is Menaechmus.

Men. But I say I am.

Men. S. (*irritated*) What yarn is this? You are Menaechmus?

Men. So I say—the son of Moschus.

Men. S. You the son of my father?

Men. No indeed, sir,—of my own; your father I have no desire to preempt or steal from you.

Mes. (*aside, after apparently profound thought*) Ye immortal gods! fulfill the unhoped-for hope I think I see before me! Yes, unless my mind deceives me, these two are the twin brothers! Yes, what they say about their country and father tallies exactly. I'll call my master aside. Menaechmus, sir!

Men.
Men. S. } What do you want?

Mes. I don't want both of you, but the one that travelled on board ship with me.

Men. I did not.

Men. S. But I did.

Mes. You're the one I want, then. (*withdrawing*) Come over here, sir.

Men. S. (*doing so*) Here I am. What is it?

Mes. (*very sagacious and important*) That man over there is either a swindler, sir, or else he's your own twin brother. For

Messenio moves SR.

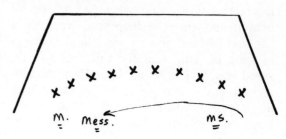

Messenio moves SL, stops center.

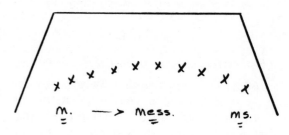

Directly to audience, no script.

Still addressing audience.

Menaechmus moves SC.

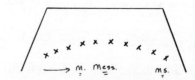

I never did see two men more alike. No drop of water, no drop of milk, is more like another, believe me, than he's like you, yes, and you like him, sir. And then he says his country and his father's name are the same as yours. We'd better go up and question him.

Men. S. By Jove, you have given me good advice! Thanks! Go on helping me, for God's sake! You are a free man if you find that he is my brother.

Mes. I hope so.

Men. S. And I—I hope so, too!

Mes. (*stepping up to Menaechmus*) Pardon me, sir. You said your name was Menaechmus, I believe.

Men. I did indeed.

Mes. This (*pointing to Menaechmus Sosicles*) gentleman's name is Menaechmus, too. You said you were born in Syracuse in Sicily; he also was born there. You said your father's name was Moschus; so was his. Now both of you can do me a good turn, and yourselves as well.

Men. You have earned my consent to any request you choose to make. Free though I am, I'll serve you quite as if you had bought and paid for me.

Mes. I have hopes, sir, of finding that you two are twin brothers, born of one mother and one father on one day.

Men. A strange statement! I wish you could bring to pass what you promise.

Mes. I can. (*tremendously earnest and subtle*) But come now, both of you, and answer my questions.

Men. Ask them when you like; I'll answer. Nothing that I know will I keep back.

Mes. Is your name Menaechmus?

Men. It is.

Mes. (*to his master*) And yours also?

Men. S. Yes.

Mes. (*to Menaechmus*) Your father was Moschus, you say?

Men. I do indeed.

Men. S. And mine, too! (*Messenio scowls at him*)

Mes. (*to Menaechmus*) Are you a Syracusan?

Men. Certainly.

Mes. (*to his master*) How about you?

Men. S. Of course I am.

MS moves SC.

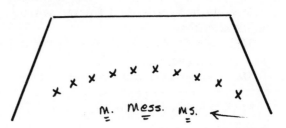

Very rapid sequence.

Mes. Everything tallies perfectly so far. Your attention further, gentlemen. (*to Menaechmus*) What is the earliest thing you remember, tell me, in your own country?

Men. Going with my father to Tarentum, his place of trade, and then straying from my father in the crowd and being carried off!

Men. S. Lord above, preserve me!

Mes. (*with asperity*) What are you bawling out for? Keep still, won't you! (*to Menaechmus*) How old were you when your father took you away from home?

Men. Seven; you see, I was just beginning to lose my first teeth. And I never saw my father after that.

Mes. What? And how many sons did your father have then?

Men. So far as I can now remember—two.

Mes. Which was the older, you or your brother?

Men. We were both of the same age.

Mes. How can that be?

Men. We were twins.

Men. S. (*unable to contain himself longer*) Oh, God has been good to me!

Mes. (*with finality*) If you interrupt, I prefer to keep still myself.

Men. S. (*contritely*) I'll keep still.

Mes. (*to Menaechmus*) Tell me, did you both have the same name?

Men. Oh no. Why, I had the same name as now, Menaechmus; he was called Sosicles then.

Men. S. (*disregarding Messenio's protest*) The proof's complete! I can't hold back—I must give him a hug! (*embracing Menaechmus*) God bless you, brother, my own twin brother! I am Sosicles!

Men. (*doubtful*) How is it then, you came to be called Menaechmus?

Men. S. After word reached us that you * * * and that our father was dead, our grandfather changed my name; he gave me yours.

Men. (*still doubtful*) No doubt this was the case. But answer me this question.

Men. S. (*eagerly*) Ask it.

Men. What was our mother's name?

Men. S. Teuximarcha.

Men. (*returning his embrace heartily*)

Right! To see you, so unhoped for, after all these years! Oh, God bless you!

Men. S. And you, too, brother! I've searched and searched for you till this moment—and a sad, weary search it's been—and now you're found I'm happy.

Mes. (*to his master*) This was how the wench here came to call you by his name; she mistook you for him, I suppose, when she invited you to lunch.

Men. (*reflecting, then frankly*) Well, well! The fact is, I did tell them to prepare lunch for me here to-day, unbeknown to my wife, whose mantle I stole from the house a while ago and gave to the wench here.

Men. S. Is this mantle I have the one you speak of, brother? (*showing it*)

Men. That's the one! How did it come into your hands?

Men. S. The wench took me in here to luncheon and said I had given it to her. Lunch I did, deuced well, and drank, and enjoyed the girl, and carried off the mantle and this piece of jewellery. (*showing bracelet*)

Men. (*laughing*) By Jove! I'm glad if you're my debtor for a bit of amusement. For when she invited you in, she took you for me.

Mes. (*to Menaechmus*) You have no objection to me being free, as you ordered, have you, sir?

Men. A perfectly just and reasonable request, brother. Grant it, for my sake.

Men. S. (*to Messenio*) Be free.

Men. Messenio, I congratulate you on your freedom!

Mes. (*ingratiatingly*) But I need better auspices to be free for good, sirs. (*waits for some hint of further benefits*)

Men. S. Now that things have turned out to our satisfaction, brother, let's both go back to our own country.

Men. As you please, brother. I'll hold an auction here and sell all I have. In the meantime let's go inside for the present, brother.

Men. S. By all means.

Mes. Do you know what I want of you, sirs?

Men. What?

Mes. To let me be auctioneer.

Men. You shall be.

Mes. Well, then, do you want it announced at once that there'll be an auction?

Men. Yes, a week from to-day.

Mes. (*bawling*) Auction . . . of the effects of Menaechmus . . . one week from to-day in the morning, mind! . . . For sale . . . slaves, household goods, land, houses . . . everything! . . . For sale . . . your own price . . . cash down! . . . For sale . . . even a wife, too . . . if any buyer appears! (*to spectators*) I don't believe the whole auction will bring more than a mere —fifty thousand pounds. Now, spectators, fare ye well and give us your loud applause. (*Exeunt Omnes*)

Menaechmus and MS move back to chairs and sit.

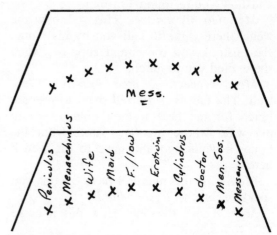

Messenio bows as cast close scripts.

Messenio moves SL as the rest of the cast rises.

They all move DS and bow.

Cast splits between Father-in-law and Erotium.

The boys take one step backward and the girls leave SL and SR followed by the boys.

Reminder: Boys' scripts in right hand as soon as they rise from their chairs—scripts hanging at arm's length.

Girls' scripts are carried in the right hand with the arm crooked.

Chapter III

CHAMBER THEATRE

DEFINED

The first point of departure in defining Chamber Theatre as contrasted to Readers' Theatre is its subject matter. Readers' Theatre concerns itself with play scripts, whereas Chamber Theatre makes use of fiction and nonfiction short stories. More use is made of the narrator because of the nature of short stories (the author interjects his own ideas from *his* point of view and motivations for actions and reactions of the characters) (Fig. 1). As we have pointed out: Readers' Theatre necessarily appears to be read;

Chamber Theatre makes use of both reading and memorization.

If your particular production of Chamber Theatre is entirely read, the audience concentration (locus) is within their minds. This was discussed in Chapter I and remains the same. If, however, you wish to incorporate memorization, then the locus is brought from the mind of your listeners onto the stage as in a regularly staged play. This generally calls for the use of costumes, special lights, sets, more movement, and business. These areas will be discussed later.

We have found that Chamber Theatre

Fig. 1. *Narrator stands apart.*

119

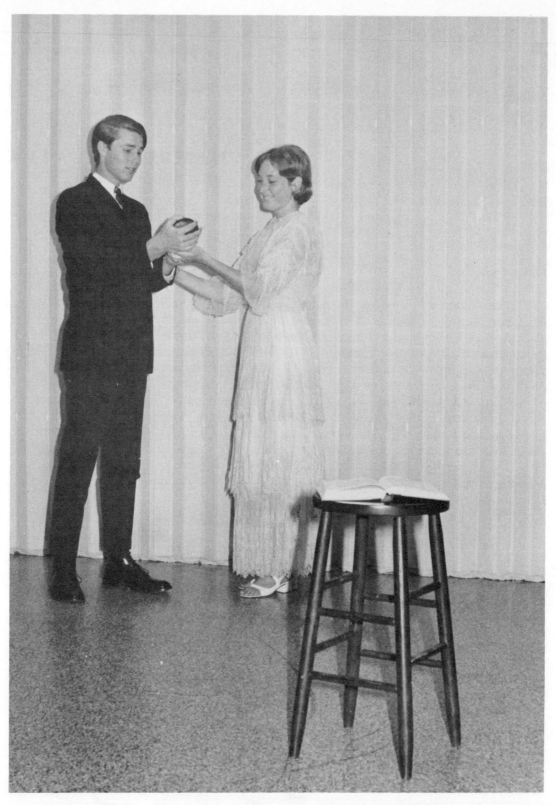

Plate X. Gift of the Magi, *Chamber Theatre, San Dieguito Union High School. Note costumes. A memorized scene, with book on stool for first-person narration.*

makes literature *live* within the classroom. It is such an exciting technique, we wonder why it is not used more often to vitalize the literature within English or American literature classrooms. The types of material applicable will be discussed further along in this chapter.

Chamber Theatre, even though it involves much of the standard staging techniques, should never be thought of as a play. Chamber Theatre has the advantage of either using the conventions of the stage—costumes, lights, scenery—or of dispensing with them. In a well-written story the description may surpass any attempt at showing costumes or scenery.

Another advantage of Chamber Theatre is the opportunity to make as much use of soliloquy as the director desires. Narrative describing a character may be spoken by that character rather than the narrator. The character *may* speak of himself in the third person as written. If he does, he may have the script readily available and pick it up and become part character and part narrator for a time. This constant return to narrative, in Chamber Theatre, proposes the motivation for actions we have seen or will see. A play or movie is generally void of this presentation of complex motivation. We often say we enjoyed the book, but the movie lacked something. That "something" the movie lacked is the author's point of view directly stated. O. Henry is a classic example of the author's point of view and motivation for character reaction being stated. The stage manager in *Our Town* and Sabina in *The Skin of Our Teeth* are examples of characters providing a point of view and motivation for character reaction through direct dialogue.

A Chamber Theatre production of a classic is far better than a dramatized adaptation in that we are able to keep more of the author's original intent intact!

Remember: *Simplicity* is the watchword! The short story or novel is not a poor stepchild of drama—learn to rely on the talent of your author. Let the novel take over and command what will be seen. You will soon learn that the novel can hold its own as a "guest upon the stage."

MOVEMENT

We will not discuss arrangement in a special section because if Chamber Theatre is entirely read, the arrangement of readers will be as it is in Readers' Theatre. If it is partly memorized, then the arrangement is not relevant but movement of characters is.

As in either of the two examples given in Chapter IV, *Editha* and *Gift of the Magi,* the direct dialogue or monologue is physically reacted to by the character or characters. Narrative parts that describe a character's subconscious thoughts are delivered by that character, not memorized but rather read and not physicalized as in standard staging of dramatic scripts. The movement of characters from reality to subconscious and back to reality must be done with extreme caution and smoothness so that the audience is fully aware of what is going on. In finishing a scene done realistically and stepping into a third-person narrative about himself, the character will step out of the scene and pick up the script at his place of reading upon the stage. As he finishes the narrative, he lays down his script, backs into his scene, meets another character, and proceeds to pick up the dialogue—realistically. The opening narrative of *The Gift of the Magi* can be read by the character of Della as effectively or more effectively than having Della react physically to the same narrative as read by a narrator. O. Henry is much more charming when it is left to the listener's imagination to construct how Della is to "flop down on the shabby little couch and howl." Della's moving from shop to shop looking for the watch fob is far more realistic within the listener's mind if Della reads the narrative.

We have chosen to discuss *The Gift of the Magi* in Chapter IV using a narrator because we felt this was more involved and would be more helpful to you. It will take very little adaptation to use Della in the role of narrator.

One general rule for movement: When you are within a scene using memorized dialogue, move in diagonals. When in a narrative and reading, you may also move parallel and perpendicular, as well as diag-

Plate XI. Gift of the Magi, *Chamber Theatre, San Dieguito Union High School. Note costumes. A memorized scene. Jim freezes while Della sits stage left and reads from script her first-person narration.*

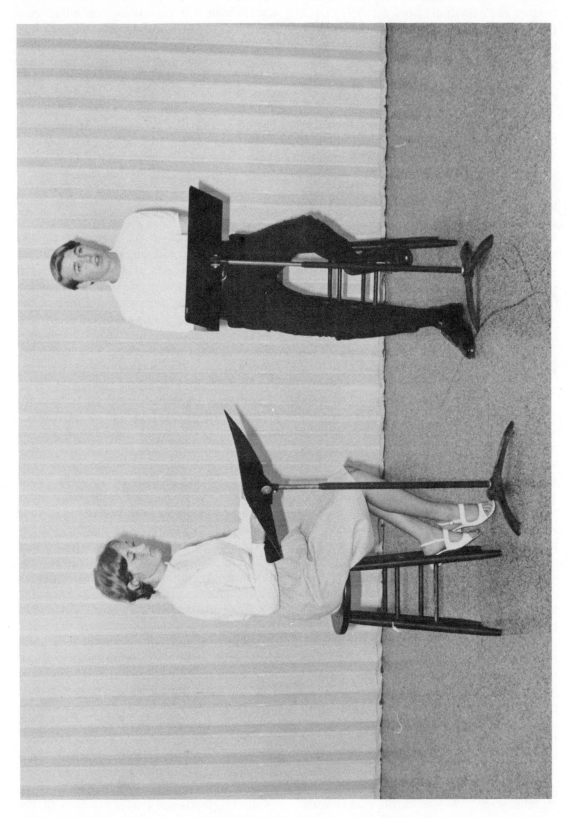

Plate XII. Gift of the Magi, Chamber Theatre, San Dieguito Union High School. Note costume idea. Both Jim and Della read from lecterns. No memorization.

onally, to the audience. A diagonal on stage is more realistic than harsh parallels or perpendiculars. Parallels, perpendiculars, arcs, and circles can be used to advantage in comedy only.

COSTUMES

Unlike Readers' Theatre in which costumes are used only to enhance and then very discreetly, Chamber Theatre allows the locus to move from the mind of the audience to the stage and back again. Therefore, unless the author has so completely and continuously described the costumes, costumes for Chamber Theatre add charm. Stage setting is minimal, so a carefully designed costume is not lost in too much to look at—a jewel in a sea of dark velvet. The costume jogs the imagination and, when the character narrates, the costume ties the past to the present or the imagination to reality.

KINDS OF MATERIAL

To be practical the best kind of material to use, at least to begin with, is a short story with considerable dialogue. With a minimum of narrative you will not be overcome with what to do with it and how to handle it. However, we suggest that you call together your group—each "armed" with a volume or two of his favorite author's short stories. Read and discuss them with the courage to move mountains. If you are "sold" on your material, nothing can keep you from a successful production.

The point of view of the story is important to consider when selecting your Chamber Theatre material. There are simply four points of view: (1) the leading character tells his story in the first person: "I remember the first day I met her . . ."; (2) a minor character tells the actions and story of the leading characters in the first person: "I remember the first time she met him . . ."; (3) an outside party looking on and telling the story of the leading characters in the third person, reporting what goes on in the minds and hearts of the leading characters: "It was during that summer when she met him that . . ." This point of

view can be read by a narrator or the character whom it is describing—in either case the third person must be maintained; and (4) the objective observer who can only speculate on the motivations and the results.

We fully expected our students to identify with only one of the four points of view. Not so! Each participant in our Chamber Theatre group felt completely at ease with every kind of material whether it was the various points of view or completely different ratios of narrative to dialogue.

REHEARSAL TECHNIQUES AND INTERPRETATION

Again, the overall success of a Chamber Theatre performance requires three initial conscientious readings of the script: quickly at first to "set" the story-line and tone of the work; the second reading will "firm up" the overall tone; and the third reading will promote ideas for production: set, costumes, staging, and those portions to be cut that can best be communicated visually.

It is well for the director to have completed all three readings and to have made many of the decisions resulting from the readings; however, the spirit of the group as an ensemble must not be dampened: Let the groups "produce" with their decisions through creativity from the very onset! Your decisions will simply help you to guide your group—not dictate.

A chamber group that has had other theatrical experience will immediately fit into meaningful interpretation of dialogue. The difficult area of Chamber Theatre is the narrative, whether done by characters within the story or by a special narrator. They all will tend to tone down narration to a point of the deadly dull news commentator. Work to overcome this honest but fatal tendency from the very start. Choric Theatre experience (Chapter V) has been a great help to our students in vitalizing the narrative portion of Chamber Theatre. Feeling the onomatopoetic value of words generally produces the facial animation necessary for any complete interpretation. "Clearly" is crisp, "Nothing" produces a negative turn of the head, "Flop" will be said with that action in mind, "Shabby" said with disdain, and howl on "Howl." "Sobs, sniffles, and smiles" must be sobbed, sniffled, and smiled. The series of such words is deadly if each word in the series is not different from the others: another excellent carryover from Choric Theatre.

It is in error that we refer to participants in Chamber Theatre as characters and narrators. It must be understood, and understood early, that the narrator must have a character. If he does not, there will be no uniformity to tie together the entire piece. Students will eventually realize that each author has his own particular style in the choice of words and their placement: character. This style-character must be reckoned with and developed to create true, enjoyable Chamber Theatre. Before the style-character of the narration is too permanently set, have several students work with all parts. The result, if your students have minds of their own, is an awareness of the variations of possible relationships between characters and narrator. A final and "right" relationship will be a revelation and the overall interest of the group will be intense and vital. When interplay between all members of the group becomes real and dynamic, a thorough analysis of the story and its purpose is the result: so satisfying and rewarding when experienced by literature classes confused with intellectualizing material rather than playing material out and making it *live*.

For extended insight into character we refer you to "Rehearsal techniques" in Chapter I. Much of the movement regulations in Chapter I apply in all types of theatre.

A true student of the theatre must learn to observe everyone and everything that surrounds him. The converse is true, a truly observant person is generally the most creative. If his interest is theatre, he is a better actor for it. How can a cook bake a cake without ingredients? She may have all the desire and talent in the world—all is in vain if she has not been serious about collecting her tools. A baseball pitcher with the potential of a Sandy Koufax can do nothing without his tools: the obvious equipment *plus* know-how to be garnered through his coach and observation. The actor cannot live a role without knowing about life and what makes it up—people.

How can an actress portray the anguish of a Mrs. Gearson in *Editha* (Chapter IV) if she has never lost a son? Perhaps she *has* experienced the empty feeling the loss in death of a pet produces—her concentration on *that* experience will produce a believable Mrs. Gearson. Perhaps the "tool" to draw upon will be her observation of a good friend who responds to a loss. Can a high-school actor feel a relationship to Willy Loman in *Death of a Salesman*? He can if he has help in constructing a "tool" by recalling past experiences that will synthesize utter despair and complete loss of hope for the future. An "F" in a required subject, a "Dear John" from his girl friend, not making the varsity squad—all these are his "tools."

Observe life—people and their environment. Learn also from the great actor who has learned that his most valuable tool is constant observation, twenty-four hours a day, seven days a week, fifty-two weeks a year.

Be sincere! Be honest! React!

Actress Geraldine Page in accepting a television Emmy Award on June 8, 1969, said, "I'm glad I had an Aunt Lulu who made the whole thing so personal to me." She *observed*, thus making her Truman Capote character live.

Chapter IV

SAMPLE LITERATURE AND NOTES FOR CHAMBER THEATRE

We will discuss two pieces of literature for Chamber Theatre: *Editha* by William Dean Howells and *The Gift of the Magi* by O. Henry. Both pieces are excellent vehicles for Chamber Theatre because the former is concerned with a problem of all time: war; and the latter is universally known and will bring pleasant remembrances for your audiences. Both can be presented with a minimum of set pieces and a simple black cyclorama.

We perhaps went to a bit more effort with *Editha* than we had to: We built a curving platform ending stage center with three steps down facing the audience. A simple parallel platform with steps on both sides—upstage and downstage—would have sufficed. It is important that the rocker for Editha's mother and the rocker for Mrs. Gearson be different and appropriate to a particular period. It is also important that the beach chairs be old and not recognizable as the easiest thing to find from someone's backyard. In *The Gift of the Magi* we used a gold gown from an earlier show and covered a chaise longue with a harmonizing, heavy, deep burnt gold. The overall color scheme was golds, browns, burnt orange, and rust. The result was a coordinated ensemble—clean and pleasing, not unlike a polished jewel set upon a rich soft pillow.

Editha offers a great deal of dialogue. *The Gift of the Magi* is generous in its narration as is the case with so many short stories—let this be a challenge.

Literature adapted for use in Chamber Theatre must not be used unless the producing group first receives permission from the author and/or publishers. Since royalties are not regularly set for production of a short story as they are for production of a play script, you will usually find that permission to use from the publisher and credit given on the program is all that is needed. Never make assumptions as to the availability of material—get your permission in writing.

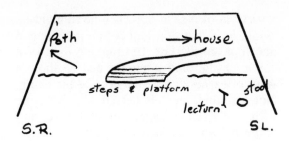

EDITHA

By William Dean Howells

The air was thick with the war feeling, like the electricity of a storm which has not yet burst. Editha sat looking out into the hot spring afternoon, with her lips parted, and panting with the intensity of the question whether she should let him go. She had decided that she could not let him stay, when she saw him at the end of the still leafless avenue, making slowly up towards the house, with his head down and his figure relaxed. She ran impatiently out on the veranda, to the edge of the steps, and imperatively demanded greater haste of him with her will before she called aloud to him: "George!"

He had quickened his pace in mystical response to her mystical urgence, before he could have heard her; [now he looked up and answered,] "Well?"

"Oh, how united we are!" [she exulted, and then she swooped down the steps to him.] "What is it?" [she cried.]

"It's war," [he said, and he pulled her up to him and kissed her.

She kissed him back intensely, but irrelevantly, as to their passion, and uttered from deep in her throat,] "How glorious!"

"It's war," [he repeated, without consenting to her sense of it; and] she did not know just what to think at first. She never knew what to think of him; that made his mystery, his charm. All through their courtship, which was contemporaneous with the growth of the war feeling, she had been puzzled by his want of seriousness about it. He seemed to despise it even more than he abhorred it. She could have understood his abhorring any sort of bloodshed; that would have been

NARRATOR (Theatre-in-the-round: the narrator circles the stage to talk to all members of the audience.)

(No narration throughout unless indicated.)

(George enters backing in, slowly, turning, observing.)

EDITHA (indicates the character delivering the quotation, throughout.)
NARRATOR (beginning: "He had . . ." (cut: ". . . now . . . answered")*
GEORGE
EDITHA
(swoops to him.)
GEORGE
(follows description.)

EDITHA
GEORGE
NARRATOR (beginning: ". . . she did not. . . ." to***.
(George moves to steps, pausing, freeze. Editha waits facing SR till George sits, then turns, freezes.)

From *Between the Dark and the Daylight* by William Dean Howells, Harper Brothers 1907, © 1907 by Harper and Brothers, © 1935 by Mildred Howells and John Mead Howells. Reprinted by permission of W. W. Howells.

* Material not spoken is in brackets. The brackets are our own.

a survival of his old life when he thought he would be a minister, and before he changed and took up the law. But making light of a cause so high and noble seemed to show a want of earnestness at the core of his being. Not but that she felt herself able to cope with a congenital defect of that sort, and make his love for her save him from himself. Now perhaps the miracle was already wrought in him. In the presence of the tremendous fact that he announced, all triviality seemed to have gone out of him; she began to feel that. He sank down on the top step, and wiped his forehead with his handkerchief, while she poured out upon him her question of the origin and authenticity of his news.

All the while, in her duplex emotioning, she was aware that now at the very beginning she must put a guard upon herself against urging him, by any word or act, to take the part that her whole soul willed him to take, for the completion of her ideal of him. He was very nearly perfect as he was, and he must be allowed to perfect himself. But he was peculiar, and he might very well be reasoned out of his peculiarity. Before her reasoning went her emotioning: her nature pulling upon his nature, her womanhood upon his manhood, without her knowing the means she was using to the end she was willing. She had always supposed that the man who won her would have done something to win her; she did not know what, but something. George Gearson had simply asked her for her love, on the way home from a concert, and she gave her love to him, without, as it were, thinking. But now, it flashed upon her, if he could do something worthy to *have* won her—be a hero, *her* hero—it would be even better than if he had done it before asking her; it would be grander. Besides, she had believed in the war from the beginning.

"But don't you see, dearest," [she said,] "that it wouldn't have come to this if it hadn't been in the order of Providence? And I call any war glorious that is for the liberation of people who have been struggling for years against the cruelest oppression. Don't you think so, too?"

"I suppose so," [he returned, languidly].

(George sits on steps. Editha turns, moves across, covering him, kneels.)

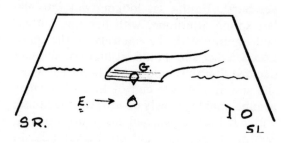

***

EDITHA (She moves beside him on steps.)

GEORGE

"But war! Is it glorious to break the peace of the world?"

"That ignoble peace! It was no peace at all, with that crime and shame at our very gates." [She was conscious of parroting the current phrases of the newspapers, but it was no time to pick and choose her words. She must sacrifice anything to the high ideal she had for him, and after a good deal of rapid argument she ended with the climax:] "But now it doesn't matter about the how or why. Since the war has come, all that is gone. There are no two sides any more. There is nothing now but our country."

[He sat with his eyes closed and his head leant back against the veranda, and he remarked, with a vague smile, as if musing aloud,] "Our country—right or wrong."

"Yes, right or wrong!" [she returned, fervidly.] "I'll go and get you some lemonade." [She rose rustling, and whisked away; when she came back with two tall glasses of clouded liquid on a tray, and the ice clucking in them, he still sat as she had left him, and she said, as if there had been no interruption:] "But there is no question of wrong in this case. I call it a sacred war. A war for liberty and humanity, if ever there was one. And I know you will see it just as I do, yet."

[He took half the lemonade at a gulp, and he answered as he set the glass down:] "I know you always have the highest ideal. When I differ from you I ought to doubt myself."

A generous sob rose in Editha's throat for the humility of a man, so very nearly perfect, who was willing to put himself below her.

Besides, she felt, more subliminally, that he was never so near slipping through her fingers as when he took that meek way.

"You shall not say that! Only, for once I happen to be right." [She seized his hand in her two hands, and poured her soul from her eyes into his.] "Don't you think so?" [she entreated him.]

[He released his hand and drank the rest of the lemonade, and she added,] "Have mine, too," [but he shook his head in answering,] "I've no business to think so, unless I act so, too."

EDITHA (Said as though memorized from another source.)

(She moves from him to DSR.)

(George follows description.)

GEORGE
EDITHA (Editha rises, moves up steps past him, exits, returns with glasses, lemonade, and tray.)

(George follows description.)

GEORGE

NARRATOR (Editha follows description.)

EDITHA
(Sits and grasps his hands in hers.)

(George follows description.)

EDITHA
GEORGE

NARRATOR

Her heart stopped a beat before it pulsed on with leaps that she felt in her neck. She had noticed that strange thing in men: they seemed to feel bound to do what they believed, and not think a thing was finished when they said it, as girls did. She knew what was in his mind, but she pretended not, [and she said,] "Oh, I am not sure," [and then faltered.]

EDITHA

[He went on as if to himself, without apparently heeding her:] "There's only one way of proving one's faith in a thing like this."

GEORGE

[She could not say that she understood, but she did understand.

He went on again.] "If I believed—if I felt as you do about the war— Do you wish me to feel as you do?"

GEORGE

[Now she was really not sure; so she said:] "George, I don't know what you mean."

EDITHA

[He seemed to muse away from her as before.] "There is a sort of fascination in it. I suppose that at the bottom of his heart every man would like at times to have his courage tested, to see how he would act."

GEORGE (moves away.)

"How can you talk in that ghastly way?"

EDITHA (still sitting.)

"It *is* rather morbid. Still, that's what it comes to, unless you're swept away by ambition or driven by conviction. I haven't the conviction or the ambition, and the other thing is what it comes to with me. I ought to have been a preacher, after all; then I couldn't have asked it of myself, as I must, now I'm a lawyer. And you believe it's a holy war, Editha?" [he suddenly addressed her.] "Oh, I know you do! But you wish me to believe so, too?"

GEORGE

(turns suddenly to face Editha.)

[She hardly knew whether he was mocking or not, in the ironical way he always had with her plainer mind. But the only thing was to be outspoken with him.]

"George, I wish you to believe whatever you think is true, at any and every cost. If I've tried to talk you into anything, I take it all back."

EDITHA (moves to him, wraps his arms about her.)

"Oh, I know that, Editha. I know how sincere you are, and how—I wish I had your undoubting spirit! I'll think it over; I'd like to believe as you do. But I don't, now; I don't, indeed. It isn't this war alone; though this seems peculiarly wanton and needless; but it's every war—so stupid; it makes me

GEORGE

sick. Why shouldn't this thing have been settled reasonably?"	
"Because," [she said, very throatily again,] "God meant it to be war."	EDITHA (turns in his arms to face him.)
"You think it was God? Yes, I suppose that is what people will say."	GEORGE
"Do you suppose it would have been war if God hadn't meant it?"	EDITHA
"I don't know. Sometimes it seems as if God had put this world into men's keeping to work it as they pleased."	GEORGE
"Now, George, that is blasphemy."	EDITHA
"Well, I won't blaspheme. I'll try to believe in your pocket Providence," [he said, and then he rose to go.]	GEORGE (releases himself and moves SR.)
"Why don't you stay to dinner?" [Dinner at Balcom's Works was at one o'clock.]	EDITHA
"I'll come back to supper, if you'll let me. Perhaps I shall bring you a convert."	GEORGE
"Well, you may come back, on that condition."	EDITHA
"All right. If I don't come, you'll understand."	GEORGE
He went away without kissing her, and she felt it a suspension of their engagement. It all interested her intensely; she was undergoing a tremendous experience, and she was being equal to it. [While she stood looking after him, her mother came out through one of the long windows onto the veranda, with a catlike softness and vagueness.]	NARRATOR (Editha looks after him absently.) (Mother enters on platform to steps.)
"Why didn't he stay to dinner?"	MOTHER
"Because—because—war has been declared." [Editha pronounced, without turning.	EDITHA
Her mother said,] "Oh, my!" [and then said nothing more until she had sat down in one of the large Shaker chairs and rocked herself for some time. Then she closed whatever tacit passage of thought there had been in her mind with the spoken words:] "Well, I hope *he* won't go."	MOTHER (moves down to rocker. Editha collects tray and glasses.) (Mother follows description.) MOTHER
"And *I* hope he *will*," [the girl said, and confronted her mother with a stormy exaltation that would have frightened any creature less unimpressionable than a cat.	EDITHA (confronting her mother stormily.)
Her mother rocked herself again for an interval of cogitation. What she arrived at in speech was:] "Well, I guess you've done a wicked thing, Editha Balcom."	(Mother follows description.) MOTHER
[The girl said, as she passed indoors through the same window her mother had	

come out by:] "I haven't done anything—yet."

[In her room, she put together all her letters and gifts from Gearson, down to the withered petals of the first flower he had offered, with that timidity of his veiled in that irony of his. In the heart of the packet she enshrined her engagement ring, which she had restored to the pretty box he had brought it her in. Then she sat down, if not calmly yet strongly, and wrote:]

George:—I understood when you left me. But I think we had better emphasize your meaning that if we cannot be one in everything we had better be one in nothing. So I am sending these things for your keeping till you have made up your mind.

I shall always love you, and therefore I shall never marry anyone else. But the man I marry must love his country first of all, and be able to say to me,

"I could not love thee, dear, so much, Loved I not honor more."

There is no honor above America with me. In this great hour there is no other honor.

Your heart will make my words clear to you. I had never expected to say so much, but it has come upon me that I must say the utmost.

Editha.

[She thought she had worded her letter well, worded it in a way that could not be bettered; all had been implied and nothing expressed.

She had it ready to send with the packet she had tied with red, white, and blue ribbon, when] it occurred to her that she was not just to him, that she was not giving him a fair chance. He said he would go and think it over, and she was not waiting. She was pushing, threatening, compelling. That was not a woman's part. She must leave him free, free, free. She could not accept for her country or herself a forced sacrifice.

In writing her letter she had satisfied the impulse from which it sprang; she could well afford to wait till he had thought it over. [She put the packet and the letter by, and rested serene in the consciousness of having done what was laid upon her by her love

EDITHA (pausing at exit off platform.)

(Mother pulls chair aside a little SL and exits as vanity and chair are set SR. Lights down SL and up SR on vanity and Editha.)

(Editha follows description.)

NARRATOR (as Editha writes.)

NARRATOR AND EDITHA

(Editha continues, Narrator fades.)

EDITHA

(Editha ends quote.)

(Editha ties red, white, and blue ribbon.)

NARRATOR (beginning ". . . it occurred to her . . . thought it over." (marked ***)

***

(Editha follows description. Lights dim, vanity off, SL lights up as SR dims. Editha moves SL to SR.)

itself to do, and yet used patience, mercy, justice.]

She had her reward. Gearson did not come to tea, but she had given him till morning, when, late at night there came up from the village the sound of a fife and drum, with a tumult of voices, in shouting, singing, and laughing. The noise drew nearer and nearer; it reached the street end of the avenue; there it silenced itself, and one voice, the voice she knew best, rose over the silence. It fell; the air was filled with cheers; the fife and drum struck up, with the shouting, singing, and laughing again, but now retreating; and a single figure came hurrying up the avenue.

She ran down to meet her lover and clung to him. He was very gay, and he put his arm round her with a boisterous laugh. "Well, you must call me Captain now; or Cap, if you prefer; that's what the boys call me. Yes, we've had a meeting at the town hall, and everybody has volunteered; and they selected me for captain, and I'm going to the war, the big war, the glorious war, the holy war ordained by the pocket Providence that blesses butchery. Come along: let's tell the whole family about it. Call them from their downy beds, father, mother, Aunt Hitty, and all the folks!"

[But when they mounted the veranda steps he did not wait for a larger audience; he poured the story out upon Editha alone.]

"There was a lot of speaking, and then some of the fools set up a shout for me. It was all going one way, and I thought it would be a good joke to sprinkle a little cold water on them. But you can't do that with a crowd that adores you. The first thing I knew I was sprinkling hell-fire on them. 'Cry havoc, and let slip the dogs of war!' That was the style. Now that it had come to the fight, there were no two parties; there was one country, and the thing was to fight to a finish as quick as possible. I suggested volunteering then and there, and I wrote my name first of all on the roster. Then they elected me—that's all. I wish I had some ice-water."

[She left him walking up and down the veranda, while she ran for the ice-pitcher and a goblet, and when she came back he

NARRATOR

(Lights grow from amber to blue but pink gel should be used on faces.)
(Noise, etc.)

(George's voice ad lib.)

(as at the opening.)

GEORGE (pink gels up)

(Move up steps, turn.)

GEORGE

(George moves down steps, ranting, pacing.)

(Editha follows description.)

was still walking up and down, shouting the story he had told her to her father and mother, who had come out more sketchily dressed than they commonly were by day. He drank goblet after goblet of the ice-water without noticing who was giving it, and kept on talking, and laughing through his talk wildly.] "It's astonishing," [he said,] "how well the worse reason looks when you try to make it appear the better. Why, I believe I was the first convert to the war in that crowd tonight! I never thought I should like to kill a man; but now I shouldn't care; and the smokeless powder lets you see the man drop that you kill. It's all for the country! What a thing it is to have a country that *can't* be wrong, but if it is, is right, anyway."

[Editha had a great, vital thought, an inspiration. She set down the ice-pitcher on the veranda floor, and ran upstairs and got the letter she had written him. When at last he noisily bade her father and mother,] "Well, good-night. I forgot I woke you up; I shan't want any sleep myself," [she followed him down the avenue to the gate. There, after the whirling words that seemed to fly away from her thoughts and refuse to serve them, she made a last effort to solemnize the moment that seemed so crazy, and pressed the letter she had written upon him.]

"What's this?" [he said.] "Want me to mail it?"

"No, no. It's for you. I wrote it after you went this morning. Keep it—keep it—and read it sometime—" [She thought, and then her inspiration came:] "Read it if ever you doubt what you've done, or fear that I regret your having done it. Read it after you've started."

They strained each other in embraces that seemed as ineffective as their words, and he kissed her face with quick, hot breaths that were so unlike him, that made her feel as if she had lost her old lover and found a stranger in his place. [The stranger said:] "What a gorgeous flower you are, with your red hair, and your blue eyes that look black now, and your face with the color painted out by the white moonshine! Let me hold you under the chin, to see whether I love blood, you tiger-lily!" [Then he laughed

(Father and mother enter.)

GEORGE

(Editha follows description during George's last speech.)

(She returns with letter.)

GEORGE
(They move SR. Dim lights SL.)

GEORGE

EDITHA

NARRATOR (to quotation)

GEORGE

(George follows description.)

Gearson's laugh, and released her, scared and giddy. Within her willfulness she had been frightened by a sense of subtler force in him, and mystically mastered as she had never been before.

She ran all the way back to the house, and mounted the steps panting. Her mother and father were talking of the great affair. Her mother said:] "Wa'n't Mr. Gearson in rather of an excited state of mind? Didn't you think he acted curious?"

"Well, not for a man who'd just been elected captain and had set 'em up for the whole of Company A," [her father chuckled back.]

"What in the world do you mean, Mr. Balcom? Oh! There's Editha!" [She offered to follow the girl indoors.]

"Don't come, mother!" [Editha called, vanishing.]

[Mrs. Balcom remained to reproach her husband.] "I don't see much of anything to laugh at."

"Well, it's catching. Caught it from Gearson. I guess it won't be much of a war, and I guess Gearson don't think so, either. The other fellows will back down as soon as they see we mean it. I wouldn't lose any sleep over it. I'm going back to bed, myself."

Gearson came again next afternoon, looking pale and rather sick, but quite himself, even to his languid irony. "I guess I'd better tell you, Editha, that I consecrated myself to your god of battles last night by pouring too many libations to him down my own throat. But I'm all right now. One has to carry off the excitement, somehow."

"Promise me," [she commanded,] "that you'll never touch it again!"

"What! Not let the cannikin clink? Not let the soldier drink? Well, I promise."

"You don't belong to yourself now; you don't even belong to *me*. You belong to your country, and you have a sacred charge to keep yourself strong and well for your country's sake. I have been thinking, thinking all night and all day long."

"You look as if you had been crying a little, too," [he said, with his queer smile.]

"That's all past. I've been thinking, and worshipping *you*. Don't you suppose I know

(Editha freezes, looking after him, as SR lights dim to blackout.)
(Lights up SL.)
MOTHER

FATHER

MOTHER (Editha moves SL.)

EDITHA

MOTHER

FATHER

(They exit. Lights fade.)

NARRATOR (Amber lights up. Editha enters running to top step, looks off, shows concern.)
(George enters.)
GEORGE

EDITHA (goes to him.)

GEORGE

EDITHA (pulls him to step.)

GEORGE

EDITHA

all that you've been through, to come to this? I've followed you every step from your old theories and opinions."

"Well, you've had a long row to hoe."

"And I know you've done this from the highest motives—"

"Oh, there won't be much pettifogging to do till this cruel war is—"

"And you haven't simply done it for my sake. I couldn't respect you if you had."

"Well, then we'll say I haven't. A man that hasn't got his own respect intact wants the respect of all the other people he can corner. But we won't go into that. I'm in for the thing now, and we've got to face our future. My idea is that this isn't going to be a very protracted struggle; we shall just scare the enemy to death before it comes to a fight at all. But we must provide for contingencies, Editha. If anything happens to me—"

"Oh, George!" [She clung to him, sobbing.]

"I don't want you to feel foolishly bound to my memory. I should hate that, wherever I happen to be."

"I am yours, for time and eternity—time and eternity." [She liked the words; they satisfied her famine for phrases.]

"Well, say eternity; that's all right; but time's another thing; and I'm talking about time. But there is something! My mother! If anything happens—"

[She winced, and he laughed.] "You're not the bold soldier-girl of yesterday!" [Then he sobered.] "If anything happens, I want you to help my mother out. She won't like my doing this thing. She brought me up to think war a fool thing as well as a bad thing. My father was in the Civil War; all through it; lost his arm in it." [She thrilled with the sense of the arm round her; what if that should be lost? He laughed as if divining her:] "Oh, it doesn't run in the family, as far as I know!" [Then he added, gravely:] "He came home with misgivings about war, and they grew on him. I guess he and mother agreed between them that I was to be brought up in his final mind about it; but that was before my time. I only knew him from my mother's report of him and his opinions; I don't know whether they were

GEORGE
EDITHA

GEORGE

EDITHA (walks DSL.)
(turns quickly to him on "I couldn't . . .")
GEORGE (paces)

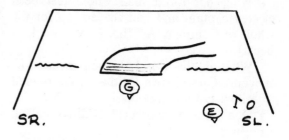

EDITHA (goes to him.)

GEORGE

EDITHA (dramatically)

GEORGE

GEORGE (follows description.)

hers first; but they were hers last. This will be a blow to her. I shall have to write and tell her—"

[He stopped, and she asked:] "Would you like me to write, too, George?"   EDITHA

"I don't believe that would do. No, I'll do   GEORGE
the writing. She'll understand a little if I say
that I thought the way to minimize it was to
make war on the largest possible scale at
once—that I felt I must have been helping
on the war somehow if I hadn't helped keep
it from coming, and I knew I hadn't; when
it came, I had no right to stay out of it."

[Whether his sophistries satisfied him or   EDITHA
not, they satisfied her. She clung to his   GEORGE
breast, and whispered, with closed eyes and
quivering lips:] "Yes, yes, yes!"

"But if anything should happen, you   EDITHA
might go to her and see what you could do   (Mother and Father enter.)
for her. You know? It's rather far off; she
can't leave her chair—"

"Oh, I'll go, if it's the ends of the earth!   GEORGE (follows description.)
But nothing will happen! Nothing *can*! I—"

[She felt herself lifted with his rising, and
Gearson was saying, with his arm still
round her, to her father:] "Well, we're off
at once, Mr. Balcom. We're to be formally
accepted at the capital, and then bunched
up with the rest somehow, and sent into
camp somewhere, and go to the front as
soon as possible. We all want to be in the
van, of course; we're the first company to
report to the Governor. I came to tell Editha,
but I hadn't got round to it."   (Blackout—exeunt.)

She saw him again for a moment at the   NARRATOR (spot up on narrator.)
capital, in the station, just before the train
started southward with his regiment. He
looked well, in his uniform, and very sol-
dierly, but somehow girlish, too, with his
clean-shaven face and slim figure. The manly
eyes and the strong voice satisfied her, and
his preoccupation with some unexpected
details of duty flattered her. Other girls were
weeping and bemoaning themselves, but she
felt a sort of noble distinction in the abstraction, the almost unconsciousness, with
which they parted. Only at the last moment   (Narrator, not George.)
he said: "Don't forget my mother. It mayn't
be such a walkover as I supposed," and he
laughed at the notion.

He waved his hand to her as the train moved off—she knew it among a score of hands that were waved to other girls from the platform of the car, for it held a letter which she knew was hers. Then he went inside the car to read it, doubtless, and she did not see him again. But she felt safe for him through the strength of what she called her love. What she called her God, always speaking the name in a deep voice and with the implication of a mutual understanding, would watch over him and keep him and bring him back to her. If with an empty sleeve, then he should have three arms instead of two, for both of hers should be his for life. She did not see, though, why she should always be thinking of the arm his father had lost.

There were not many letters from him, but they were such as she could have wished, and she put her whole strength into making hers such as she imagined he could have wished, glorifying and supporting him. She wrote to his mother glorifying him as their hero, but the brief answer she got was merely to the effect that Mrs. Gearson was not well enough to write herself, and thanking her for her letter by the hand of someone who called herself "Yrs truly, Mrs. W. J. Andrews."

Editha determined not to be hurt, but to write again quite as if the answer had been all she expected. Before it seemed as if she could have written, there came news of the first skirmish, and in the list of the killed, which was telegraphed as a trifling loss on our side, was Gearson's name. There was a frantic time of trying to make out that it might be, must be, some other Gearson; but the name and the company and the regiment and the State were too definitely given.

Then there was a lapse into depths out of which it seemed as if she never could rise again; then a lift into clouds far above all grief, black clouds, that blotted out the sun, but where she soared with him, with George—George! She had the fever that she expected of herself, but she did not die in it; she was not even delirious, and it did not last long. When she was well enough to leave her bed, her one thought was of George's mother, of his strangely worded

(Vanity and chair on SR.)

(Lights SR up dim. Editha at vanity reading and writing.)

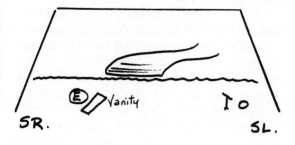

(Mother enters. Pantomime talking, Editha reacts, swoons, lights dim.)

wish that she should go to her and see what she could do for her. In the exaltation of the duty laid upon her—it buoyed her up instead of burdening her—she rapidly recovered.

Her father went with her on the long railroad journey from Northern New York to Western Iowa; he had business out at Davenport, and he said he could just as well go then as any other time; and he went with her to the little country town where George's mother lived in a little house on the edge of the illimitable cornfields, under trees pushed to a top of a rolling prairie. George's father had settled there after the Civil War, as so many other old soldiers had done; but they were Eastern people, and Editha fancied touches of the East in the June roses overhanging the front door, and the garden with early summer flowers stretching from the gate of the paling fence.

It was very low inside the house, and so dim, with the closed blinds, that they could scarcely see one another: Editha tall and black in her crapes which filled the air with the smell of their dyes; her father standing decorously apart with his hat on his forearm, as at funerals; a woman rested in a deep armchair, and the woman who had let the strangers in stood behind the chair.

[The seated woman turned her head round and up, and asked the woman behind her chair:] "*Who* did you say?"

Editha, if she had done what she expected of herself, would have gone down on her knees at the feet of the seated figure and said, "I am George's Editha," for answer.

But instead of her own voice she heard that other woman's voice, [saying:] "Well, I don't know as I *did* get the name just right. I guess I'll have to make a little more light in here," [and she went and pushed two of the shutters ajar.

Then Editha's father said, in his public will-now-address-a-few-remarks tone:] "My name is Balcom, ma'am—Junius H. Balcom, of Balcom's Works, New York; my daughter—"

"Oh!" [the seated woman broke in, with a powerful voice, the voice that always surprised Editha from Gearson's slender frame.] "Let me see you. Stand round where the light

(Vanity is off, set up SR with chair, end table, and an item or two which will represent an earlier era. Mrs. Gearson, woman, Editha, and Father enter.)

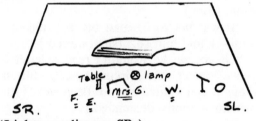

(Lights up dim on SR.)

MRS. GEARSON
NARRATOR

(Narrator, not Editha.)

WOMAN

(Woman follows description.)
(Lights brighter.)

FATHER

MRS. GEARSON

can strike on your face," [and Editha dumbly obeyed.] "So, you're Editha Balcom," [she sighed.]

"Yes," [Editha said, more like a culprit than a comforter.]   EDITHA

"What did you come for?" [Mrs. Gearson asked.   MRS. GEARSON

Editha's face quivered and her knees shook.] "I came—because—because George —" [She could go no further.]   EDITHA

"Yes," [the mother said,] "he told me he had asked you to come if he got killed. You didn't expect that, I suppose, when you sent him."   MRS. GEARSON

"I would rather have died myself than done it!" [Editha said, with more truth in her deep voice than she ordinarily found in it.] "I tried to leave him free—"   EDITHA

"Yes, that letter of yours, that came back with his other things, left him free."   MRS. GEARSON

[Editha saw now where George's irony came from.]

"It was not to be read before—unless— until—I told him so," [she faltered.]   EDITHA

"Of course, he wouldn't read a letter of yours, under the circumstances, till he thought you wanted him to. Been sick?" [the woman abruptly demanded.]   MRS. GEARSON

"Very sick," [Editha said, with self-pity.]   EDITHA
"Daughter's life," [her father interposed,]   FATHER
"was almost despaired of, at one time."

[Mrs. Gearson gave him no heed.] "I suppose you would have been glad to die, such a brave person as you! I don't believe *he* was glad to die. He was always a timid boy, that way; he was afraid of a good many things; but if he was afraid, he did what he made up his mind to. I suppose he made up his mind to go, but I knew what it cost him by what it cost me when I heard of it. I had been through *one* war before. When you sent him you didn't expect he would get killed."   MRS. GEARSON

[The voice seemed to compassionate Editha, and it was time.] "No," she huskily murmured.   EDITHA

"No, girls don't; women don't, when they give their men up to their country. They think they'll come marching back, some-how, just as gay as they went, or if it's an empty sleeve, or even an empty pantaloon   MRS. GEARSON it's all the more glory, and they're so much the prouder of them, poor things!"

[The tears began to run down Editha's face; she had not wept till then; but it was now such a relief to be understood that the tears came.]

"No, you didn't expect him to get killed," [Mrs. Gearson repeated, in a voice which was startlingly like George's again.] "You just expected him to kill someone else, some of those foreigners, that weren't there because they had any say about it, but because they had to be there, poor wretches—conscripts, or whatever they call 'em. You thought it would be all right for my George, *your* George, to kill the sons of those miserable mothers and the husbands of those girls that you would never see the faces of." [The woman lifted her powerful voice in a psalmlike note.] "I thank my God he didn't live to do it! I thank my God they killed him first, and that he ain't livin' with their blood on his hands!" [She dropped her eyes, which she had raised with her voice, and glared at Editha.] "What you got that black on for?" [She lifted herself by her powerful arms so high that her helpless body seemed to hang limp its full length.] "Take it off, take it off, before I tear it from your back!"

The lady who was passing the summer near Balcom's Works was sketching Editha's beauty, which lent itself wonderfully to the effects of a colorist. It had come to that confidence which is rather apt to grow between artist and sitter, and Editha had told her everything.

"To think of your having such a tragedy in your life!" [the lady said. She added:] "I suppose there are people who feel that way about war. But when you consider the good this war has done—how much it has done for the country! I can't understand such people, for my part. And when you had come all the way out there to console her—got up out of a sickbed! Well!"

"I think," [Editha said, magnanimously,] "she wasn't quite in her right mind; and so did papa."

"Yes," [the lady said, looking at Editha's

(Editha follows description.)

MRS. GEARSON

(Follow description.)

(Fade to blackout.)
(Spot up on narrator.)
NARRATOR (beach chairs with Editha and lady sitting, follow description.)

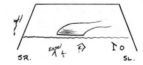

LADY

EDITHA

LADY

lips in nature and then at her lips in art, and giving an empirical touch to them in the picture.] "But how dreadful of her! How perfectly—excuse me—how *vulgar!*"

A light broke upon Editha in the darkness which she felt had been without a gleam of brightness for weeks and months. The mystery that had bewildered her was solved by the word; and from that moment she rose from groveling in shame and self-pity, and began to live again in the ideal.

NARRATOR (lights fade to blackout before narrator finishes.)

THE GIFT OF THE MAGI

By O. Henry

One dollar and eighty-seven cents. That was all. And sixty cents of it was in pennies. Pennies saved one and two at a time by bull-dozing the grocer and the vegetable man and the butcher until one's cheeks burned with the silent imputation of parsimony that such close dealing implied. Three times Della counted it. One dollar and eighty-seven cents. And the next day would be Christmas.

There was clearly nothing to do but flop down on the shabby little couch and howl. So Della did it. Which instigates the moral reflection that life is made up of sobs, sniffles, and smiles, with sniffles predominating.

While the mistress of the home is gradually subsiding from the first stage to the second, take a look at the home. A furnished flat at $8 per week. It did not exactly beggar description, but it certainly had that word on the lookout for the mendicancy squad.

In the vestibule below was a letterbox into which no letter would go, and an electric button from which no mortal finger could coax a ring. Also appertaining thereunto was a card bearing the name "Mr. James Dillingham Young."

The "Dillingham" had been flung to the breeze during a former period of prosperity when its possessor was being paid $30 per week. Now, when the income was shrunk to $20, the letters of "Dillingham" looked blurred, as though they were thinking seriously of contracting to a modest and unassuming D. But whenever Mr. James Dillingham Young came home and reached his flat above he was called "Jim" and greatly hugged by Mrs. James Dillingham Young, already introduced to you as Della. Which is all very good.

Della finished her cry and attended to her

From *The Complete Works of O. Henry.* Permission granted for reprinting by Doubleday and Company, Inc., publishers.

The keyword for *The Gift of the Magi* is simplicity. Keep to an absolute minimum of stage setting. We have had the greatest success with O. Henry's masterpiece in theatre-in-the-round. It is easily adapted, however, to the proscenium stage.

We used a chaise longue with the "scroll" end. It had been covered in velvet and so when we recovered it in burnt gold we left the original covering for added padding and also to "hold" the new material. Since the chaise was Victorian we used a small Victorian chair with the round seat and back. A Victorian marble-topped table completed the "set." All other set pieces that Della would normally have are used in pantomime.

The NARRATOR is an important part of the script since the dialogue is so minimal. This is *not* a disadvantage—make the most of the style of pantomime. There is plenty to do during the narration.

Paragraph #1: Della counts her change three times: twice in this paragraph and once in paragraph #3.

Paragraph #2: She cries (with restraint).

Paragraph #3: Count the change the third time.

Paragraph #4: Gather the coins and deposit them into a little velvet sack.

Paragraph #5: Reflect on "Jim" and respond to the narration.

Paragraph #6: Follow the narration.

cheeks with the powder rag. She stood by the window and looked out dully at a gray cat walking a gray fence in a gray backyard. Tomorrow would be Christmas Day, and she had only $1.87 with which to buy Jim a present. She had been saving every penny she could for months, with this result. Twenty dollars a week doesn't go far. Expenses had been greater than she had calculated. They always are. Only $1.87 to buy a present for Jim. Her Jim. Many a happy hour she had spent planning for something nice for him. Something fine and rare and sterling—something just a little bit near to being worthy of the honor of being owned by Jim.

There was a pier-glass between the windows of the room. Perhaps you have seen a pier-glass in an $8 flat. A very thin and very agile person may, by observing his reflection in a rapid sequence of longitudinal strips, obtain a fairly accurate conception of his looks. Della, being slender, had mastered the art.

Suddenly she whirled from the window and stood before the glass. Her eyes were shining brilliantly, but her face had lost its color within twenty seconds. Rapidly she pulled down her hair and let it fall to its full length.

Now, there were two possessions of the James Dillingham Youngs in which they both took a mighty pride. One was Jim's gold watch that had been his father's and his grandfather's. The other was Della's hair. Had the Queen of Sheba lived in the flat across the airshaft, Della would have let her hair hang out the window some day to dry just to depreciate Her Majesty's jewels and gifts. Had King Solomon been the janitor, with all his treasures piled up in the basement, Jim would have pulled out his watch every time he passed just to see him pluck at his beard from envy.

So now Della's beautiful hair fell about her, rippling and shining like a cascade of brown waters. It reached below her knee and made itself almost a garment for her. And then she did it up again nervously and quickly. Once she faltered for a minute and stood still while a tear or two splashed on the worn red carpet.

Della catches reflection in pier-glass.
Wipes it off.
She observes her reflection critically.

Della pauses and suddenly remembers something. Goes to the window.
She whirls from the window; returns to the glass.

Lets her hair down.

During this narration she arranges and re-arranges her hair.

Act out the drying of her hair.

Charmingly like Jim, she acts out the looking at the watch.

Return to the examination of the hair.

Twists it up again into the topknot.

On went her old brown jacket; on went her old brown hat. With a whirl of skirts and with the brilliant sparkle still in her eyes, she fluttered out the door and down the stairs to the street.

Where she stopped the sign read: "Mme. Sofronie. Hair Goods of All Kinds." One flight up Della ran, and collected herself, panting. Madame, large, too white, chilly, hardly looked the "Sofronie."

"Will you buy my hair?" [asked Della.]*

"I buy hair," [said Madame.] "Take yer hat off and let's have a sight at the looks of it."

[Down rippled the brown cascade.]

"Twenty dollars," [said Madame, lifting the mass with a practised hand.]

"Give it to me quick," [said Della.]

Oh, the next two hours tripped by on rosy wings. Forget the hashed metaphor. She was ransacking the stores for Jim's present.

She found it at last. It surely had been made for Jim and no one else. There was no other like it in any of the stores, and she had turned all of them inside out. It was a platinum fob chain simple and chaste in design, properly proclaiming its value by substance alone and not by meretricious ornamentation—as all good things should do. It was even worthy of The Watch. As soon as she saw it she knew that it must be Jim's. It was like him. Quietness and value—the description applied to both. Twenty-one dollars they took from her for it, and she hurried home with the 87 cents. With that chain on his watch Jim might be properly anxious about the time in any company. Grand as the watch was, he sometimes looked at it on the sly on account of the old leather strap that he used in place of a chain.

When Della reached home her intoxication gave way a little to prudence and reason. She got out her curling irons and lighted the gas and went to work repairing the ravages made by generosity added to love. Which is always a tremendous task, dear friends—a mammoth task.

Within [forty] minutes her head was cov-

She dresses for the street.

Take rapid turns about the stage simulating the descent down the stairs.

DELLA (then narrator continues.)
She circles the stage in a smaller sweep. Madame has entered and uses the chaise, table, and chair.
DELLA
MADAME

No narration.
MADAME (follows description.)

DELLA (remove hair fall. Lights fade.)
NARRATOR
Retraces steps and approaches the outer edge of the stage five times, not in adjacent segments but crossing the major portion of the stage each time. The buying will be in pantomime.

Let us see just how lovely the fob is through the facial expression.

Pays the twenty-one dollars in the blackout. Now she uses invisible money so that the store clerk is eliminated from the cast. If he is real, the other four must be real too.

Retraces steps home.

Curling iron business. Her hair has been curled and brushed as straight as possible before the fall was attached. Now she can pantomime the curling and when it's brushed the hair will curl.

Cut "forty."

---

* Cut bracketed material.

ered with tiny, close-lying curls that made her look wonderfully like a truant schoolboy. She looked at her reflection in the mirror long, carefully, and critically.

Pier-glass reflection business.

DELLA

"If Jim doesn't kill me," [she said to herself,] "before he takes a second look at me, he'll say I look like a Coney Island chorus girl. But what could I do—oh! what could I do with a dollar and eighty-seven cents?"

At 7 o'clock the coffee was made and the frying-pan was on the back of the stove, hot and ready to cook the chops.

NARRATOR
Cooking business.

Jim was never late. Della doubled the fob chain in her hand and sat on the corner of the table near the door that he always entered. Then she heard his step on the stair away down on the first flight, and she turned white for just a moment. She had a habit of saying little silent prayers about the simplest everyday things, [and now she whispered:] "Please God, make him think I am still pretty."

Della "arranges" herself for Jim's entrance.

Let us "hear" Jim through Della's expression.
Panic.
Prayer.

DELLA

[The door opened and Jim stepped in and closed it. He looked thin and very serious. Poor fellow, he was only twenty-two—and to be burdened with a family! He needed a new overcoat and he was without gloves.

Jim enters.

Let him take off his coat etc. before he sees Della; on the steps up.

Jim stopped inside the door, as immovable as a setter at the scent of quail. His eyes were fixed upon Della, and there was an expression in them that she could not read, and it terrified her. It was not anger, nor surprise, nor disapproval, nor horror, nor any of the sentiments that she had been prepared for. He simply stared at her fixedly with that peculiar expression on his face.

Follow description.

Beautiful possibilities of communication without words.

Della wriggled off the table and went to him.]

"Jim, darling," [she cried,] "don't look at me that way. I had my hair cut off and sold it because I couldn't have lived through Christmas without giving you a present. It'll grow out again—you won't mind, will you? I just had to do it. My hair grows awfully fast. Say 'Merry Christmas!' Jim, and let's be happy. You don't know what a nice— what a beautiful, nice gift I've got for you."

DELLA

Business of making her hair as lovely as possible—fluff it, try to be proud of it.

"You've cut off your hair?" [asked Jim, laboriously, as if he had not arrived at that patent fact yet even after the hardest mental labor.]

JIM

"Cut it off and sold it," [said Della.]

DELLA

"Don't you like me just as well, anyhow? I'm me without my hair, ain't I?"

[Jim looked about the room curiously.]

"You say your hair is gone?" [he said, with an air almost of idiocy.]

"You needn't look for it," [said Della.] "It's sold, I tell you—sold and gone, too. It's Christmas Eve, boy. Be good to me, for it went for you. Maybe the hairs of my head were numbered," [she went on with a sudden serious sweetness,] "but nobody could ever count my love for you. Shall I put the chops on, Jim?"

Out of his trance Jim seemed quickly to wake. He enfolded his Della. For ten seconds let us regard with discreet scrutiny some inconsequential object in the other direction. Eight dollars a week or a million a year—what is the difference? A mathematician or a wit would give you the wrong answer. The magi brought valuable gifts, but that was not among them. This dark assertion will be illuminated later on.

Jim drew a package from his overcoat pocket and threw it upon the table.

"Don't make any mistake, Dell," [he said,] "about me. I don't think there's anything in the way of a haircut or a shave or a shampoo that could make me like my girl any less. But if you'll unwrap that package you may see why you had me going a while at first."

White fingers and nimble tore at the string and paper. And then an ecstatic scream of joy; and then, alas! a quick feminine change to hysterical tears and wails, necessitating the immediate employment of all the comforting powers of the lord of the flat.

For there lay The Combs—the set of combs, side and back, that Della had worshipped for long in a Broadway window. Beautiful combs, pure tortoise shell, with jewelled rims—just the shade to wear in the beautiful vanished hair. They were expensive combs, she knew, and her heart had simply craved and yearned over them without the least hope of possession. And now, they were hers, but the tresses that should have adorned the coveted adornments were gone.

But she hugged them to her bosom, and at length she was able to look up with dim

---

(follows description.)
JIM

DELLA

NARRATOR
She doesn't move. He takes her comfortingly. They freeze embrace through narration.

Follow description—make the "threw" gentle.
JIM

NARRATOR
Follow description.

DELLA

ad lib

Della needs to take them from the package so that the audience may see.

She starts to put them in her hair until she feels that there is so little there!

Follow description.

eyes and a smile [and say:] "My hair grows so fast, Jim!"

[And then Della leaped up like a little singed cat and cried,] "Oh, oh!"

[Jim had not seen his beautiful present. She held it out to him eagerly upon her open palm. The dull precious metal seemed to flash with a reflection of her bright and ardent spirit.]

"Isn't it a dandy, Jim? I hunted all over town to find it. You'll have to look at the time a hundred times a day now. Give me your watch. I want to see how it looks on it."

[Instead of obeying, Jim tumbled down on the couch and put his hands under the back of his head and smiled.]

"Dell," [said he,] "let's put our Christmas presents away and keep 'em a while. They're too nice to use just at present. I sold the watch to get the money to buy your combs. And now suppose you put the chops on."

The magi, as you know, were wise men—wonderfully wise men—who brought gifts to the Babe in the manger. They invented the art of giving Christmas presents. Being wise, their gifts were no doubt wise ones, possibly bearing the privilege of exchange in case of duplication. And here I have lamely related to you the uneventful chronicle of two foolish children in a flat who most unwisely sacrificed for each other the greatest treasures of their house. But in a last word to the wise of these days let it be said that of all who give gifts these two were the wisest. Of all who give and receive gifts, such as they, are wisest. Everywhere they are wisest. They are the magi.

DELLA

Follow description.
DELLA

Let the chain fall from the hand.

DELLA

Long pause. Smile comes slowly over Jim's face. Follow description.

JIM

Pause after "present"—Della questions his words, then he continues.
NARRATOR
Their reactions to their plight are *slowly* revealed during this narration.

Leave the audience with no question about the undying love Jim and Della hold for each other. A restrained but complete embrace beginning . . .
. . ."Of all. . . ."

Pause after "wisest."
They release each other. Jim still holds Della's face in his hands, cupping her jaws in his hands with his fingertips on her ears. His fingertips move slowly down to her chin. Della takes Jim's face in her hands and kisses him gently on
"They are the magi."

Lights fade to blackout.

Chapter V

CHORIC THEATRE

DEFINED

Please! Choric Theatre is *not* a fearsome activity! If once you experiment with it, you will be caught up in its appeal. Some formal training is a definite advantage; it is not a requirement for someone who already has theatre "in the blood" and some theatre training. We can think of times when various forms of formal training in any art form is a definite hindrance—not allowing you to go against the "rules" or to try something that has been "proved" impossible. Let us hasten to add that in most cases the rules should be firmly set in the mind before they are broken—then when you break them, you have reason rather than ignorance. The senior scientist has failed to achieve in some areas because he *is* a senior and knows that a particular problem has been proven unsolvable. The junior scientist tries and succeeds—because he does not know that "it cannot be done."

Choric Theatre is our all-inclusive term for group interpretation generally called Verse Choir or Choric Speech. Choric is in the manner of chorus. The origin of "choric" is the Greek word "chorikos": belonging to a choral dance. Our name for our particular group is Drama Chorōs. Chorōs is Greek: a dance in a ring, a chorus. Both terms, then, "choric" and "chorōs" include dance and chorus. Dance is interpretive movement, and chorus is a number of people singing or speaking something together simultaneously. We think "Verse Choir" or "Choric Speech" are limiting in definition. "Verse" seems to eliminate other material, and "Choir" (as "chorus") is unimaginative and too synonymous with singing. "Speech" eliminates the possibilities that "Drama" or "Theatre" inspire. Drama Chorōs, then, is any form of material delivered in the manner of group speaking with interpretive movement. We must give credit where credit is due—our name is borrowed from Mary Gwen Owen and her magnificently alive group, The Macalester College Drama Chorōs of St. Paul, Minnesota.

ARRANGEMENT OF READERS

Included in these few pages are photographs of our Drama Chorōs. Positions shown are basic and can complement one another within a given performance. They most definitely should be but a starting point for your Choric Theatre group. The imaginations of the entire group must be allowed to create in everything you do. As in Readers' Theatre there is a basic arrangement (Fig. 1) that is the easiest and best to promote group interpretation: the whole group standing in their assigned voice-quality sections.

We have our Drama Chorōs divided into three groups: dark voices, placed center, generally only boys; medium voices, placed stage left (to the left of the dark voices); and light voices, placed stage right (to the right of the dark voices).

An arrangement for large numbers is that of placing voices in chromatic order: dark voices to stage right, medium-dark next,

Fig. 1. *Basic arrangement.*

then medium, medium-light, light, and very light. You will probably start, at least, with three groupings; or, if you work with elementary boys and girls, you will have only one grouping.

Basic to the chorus arrangement is that the group is not cramped. Try to avoid doing with less space than you need. Make arrangements to use the choir risers until you can have a set or two of your own. Arrange your people in even and odd numbers—six in the first row, five or seven in the second, then six, then five or seven; in this way each member can look between the heads and over the adjacent shoulders of the people standing in the next row down (Fig. 2). If

Fig. 2. *Basic arrangement for sightlines.*

scripts are used either as props or out of necessity—and we have discussed the merit of scripts—you may have to use three rows: first row on the main floor and a foot and

a half forward of the first step of the risers, the second row on the first step, and the third row on the *third* step. This allows room to hold a script properly.

MOVEMENT

As shown in Plates XIII, XIV, XV, we try to take a different position every three or four numbers. A third position uses stools at random within eight to twelve feet in front of the risers. Some members sit on the risers, some on stools, and some on the floor. Others stand behind the risers and behind stools farther to stage right and stage left. This is a good position for the *Shaggy Stories* (Chapter VI), with the storyteller sitting center and part of the group sitting in front of him with their backs to the audience, pivoting toward the audience to deliver comments.

One of the most important techniques of movement is that everyone move at once and with much vitality. We usually bow after each number and always before we move to a new position. The bow sets the rhythm for the move. The most attractive kind of move is for each member to take one step backward before turning to move to another position. This move softens the harsh look of an abrupt turn, which *can* look like rejection.

To enter the stage at the beginning of a program, we like to run, generally from both sides of the auditorium down the aisles. In our theatre-in-the-round we have used three or all four aisles. We have never used full

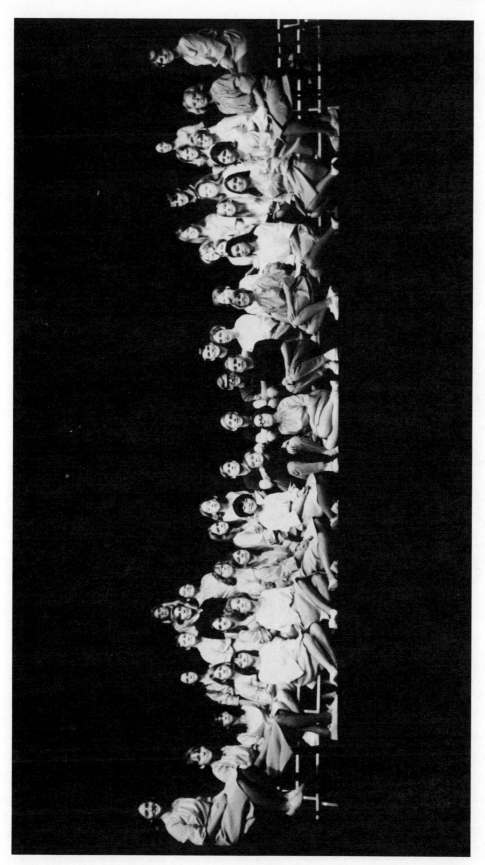

Plate XIII. *Basic seating arrangement.*

Plate XIV. *Specialty group.*

Plate XV. *Drama Chorós, San Dieguito Union High School. Our first costumes: navy skirts and trousers, light-blue shirts and blouses with patches.*

round—only three-quarter. Running makes your group vital—exciting and unified. As they move from position to position, they will add little catch-steps—almost a hop or jump—to propel them on their way. Result: vim and vigor! Caution your group never to stop and wait. If some cannot keep moving on their way back to the risers or on an exit, they must take the long way around—walk rapidly and with purpose but in the opposite direction—then circle around and head toward their destination. On a proscenium stage those on stage right exit left and those on stage left exit right. In the round we ask them to exit by the aisle farthest from their starting point. If at least half of the group does this, much interest and intrigue is added. This avoids "pile-ups." One final rule: When moving, do not leave it all up to your legs; move rapidly and with your whole body.

COSTUMES, LIGHTS, AND STAGE DESIGN

Costumes. Our first major public performance with the Drama Chorōs was looked upon with most eager anticipation. Of course we wanted to look as "costumed" as possible. This was a guest appearance with San Diego State College Verse Choir and the Macalester Drama Chorōs. The Verse Choir appeared in beautiful blue and deep red choir robes and stoles and the Macalester group in Scotch plaid motif—kilts, long skirts. Having a budget comparing to the income of a child's lemonade stand, we did the best we could. We had a supply of felt stick-on patches bearing our department name and crest in blue and white, so light blue shirts and blouses and navy blue trousers and skirts were chosen. The only major error was the lengths of the skirts—and it was major! Therefore, our earlier word of warning: middle-of-the-knee-length skirts!

Since our first "costume" we have managed attire that is practical and attractive. We bought patterns—one of each size—and the girls made their own light blue brushed denim wraparound skirts. They also made peasant blouses of red and white check. The sleeves are long and they can wear them that way or three-quarter bell—we prefer

Plate XVI. *Drama Chorōs, San Dieguito Union High School. Note black skirts and trousers, cardigans, black pullovers with pearls.*

the bell style. The skirts were cut with a hem of at least six inches so that they can be easily altered. The widths were cut as large as possible—also allowing for later use. The boys bought their own light blue denim jeans, and they alternate shirts: Sometimes they wear navy blue; at other times they wear white. The navy blue can be Banlon golf shirts, turtleneck, or sweaters—anything, just so the color is right. The white is a short-sleeved button-down. We made handkerchiefs of the check material to be carried in the right hip pocket with either navy or white. With the white shirts we add a checkered neckerchief. Everyone wears white deck shoes. The shoes are quiet, slip-proof, and add bounce. We now wish we had lined the skirts with the red-and-white-check material —even though altering would have been more difficult. You will notice some girls in white blouses. The reason is to break up what could become too much red and white and to be interesting.

Our dancers wear red leotards, white blouses or shirts, and a red-and-white-checkered cummerbund.

For more serious programs we cut out all red and white, and wear white shirts and blouses with the department patch, and black shoes.

Our next project will be full-length black skirts gathered at the waist, whipped-cream-white blouses, and cummerbunds of various colors. The cummerbunds will be worn in various combinations: all green; all blue; all yellow; all gold; all rust; green and blue; gold and rust; red, white, and blue; and in time each person can wear an entirely different color or shade—Mardi Gras! The boys will wear white turtleneck sweaters and black trousers or tuxedos.

Again, do not overlook borrowing robes from the school choir, athletic or music blazers, all cardigan sweaters—any color, or all sweat shirts—any color. Look around. Beg or borrow—if all else fails, buy!

Lights. Lighting can be as creative or as simple as you wish, but light it must be. Again, back-light so scripts are easily read and faces are lit from script reflection.

So few times occur when we use a soloist for any great period of time that we have never arranged for special lighting on single persons. Even in the case of the *Shaggy Stories* we would not want to solo-light because the facial response of the chorōs and their comments are so essential to the general success of the stories.

We treat the chorōs as one, and shy from featuring individuals. We do not depend on individuals for solo parts but rather multi-cast all solo parts. In this way everyone is a soloist. Therefore, no attempt is made to single out individuals with lights—only voices and the message.

A general dimming of lights for more serious selections or changes in background color for variations in mood can be made. A popular color for mood pieces is blue. Try for more originality; and when color *is* used, arrange for the faces to remain in neutral pink. The colors in your costumes will help to determine light colors. Colors must complement each other and so the pink complements the face, making it healthy, not sick. Facial shadows are a startling effect for some material. Take another look at the *Faustus* chorus in Chapter I.

Stage design. The rapidity in change of theme and mood in Choric Theatre prohibits involved, heavily constructed sets. Quick-change effects such as shadows and color from lighting are the most effectual for Choric Theatre. The various arrangements of personnel will help set mood in a kind of human set design.

Probably the best design should come from the performance itself. Take, for instance, Doris Steffy's *Take My Hand*. A startlingly effective design was managed midway through the poem by displaying simulated American flags, which had been hidden in the waistbands of the costumes. We divided the chorōs into thirds—one group had white flags, another blue, and the third red. The flags themselves were longer than the 6-inch staffs, making the flow a continuous mass of waving red, white, and blue. After they were used they were easily "palmed" by rolling the staff with one hand and holding the material end in the other hand. Before they were abandoned, they were used as teachers' pointers, and then to point with, as "the black boy stands alone."

Plate XVII. *Choric Theatre, specialty group, San Dieguito Union High School. Note sweat shirts of various colors, neckerchiefs, bandanas, and leotards.*

In carnival sequences of poems, have multicolored balloons hidden in the waistband. While one or two people attract attention with a solo or duet, everyone else turns his back to the audience and inflates his balloon. After they are waved, they can be deflated and returned to their "hiding spot." Be careful that the clever ideas do not become so clever that they destroy an important message. It is far better to do without stage design than to take unnecessary time to "set up" sets, even though they may be meaningful or symbolic. Here again justify simplicity by putting the locus in the mind of the beholder. Do not let your readers depend on stage design and/or lights for mood—their talent must be used to promote mood!

Kinds of Material

Practically any piece of literature can be done in Choric Theatre if it is not too long and/or has sufficient variety within itself. *These I Have Loved* by Rupert Brooke is packed with imagery and demands more from a group than many can give it. If it is cut judiciously for a particular performing group, it is highly successful. Just about everything written by Robert Frost is perfect for Choric Theatre. Ogden Nash and Dorothy Parker offer great quantities of material that are relished by both performers and audiences of any age. Familiar soliloquies from Shakespeare are educational and, of course, offer vast opportunities for variety in rhythm and voice qualities. We look for an abundance of descriptive words and phrases so that the onomatopoetic qualities can be expressed. Our chorōs is particularly enthusiastic about *Custard the Dragon* by Nash. Words such as "growled," "cried," "sharp," and "daggers" are fun to overplay. We "tell it like it is": a kindergarten teacher reading to five-year-olds—"wide-eyed and bushy-tailed."

It is wise in Choric Theatre programs to "rest" the group midway through the program. We use the *Shaggy Stories* as "breathers" and a story that seems to be used a great deal by scouting groups and Campfire Girls: *The Lion Hunt.* In *The Lion Hunt* a soloist from the group tells the story with actions, and the audience responds as an impromptu verse choir. He begins, "Do you want to go on a lion hunt?" The audience repeats, "Do you want to go on a lion hunt?" Soloist, "O.K. Let's go!" As he says this, he begins slapping his thighs quite rapidly. The audience repeats the words, "O.K. Let's go!" and also does the hand movements. Then, "Not so fast; this is Africa, you know." The audience repeats the sentence and they all slow down the hand movements. It is a very simple number and one that is easy for the audience to follow. It makes them feel a part of the program. Generally we have the chorōs divide and run down the aisles and spread themselves among the audience; then they can become part of the audience and encourage participation. This technique not only rests them but gets them closer to their audience in a most delightful way.

Another source of excellent material is the Japanese haiku. Originally haiku was the first three lines of the tanka, a five-line poem. Haiku totals seventeen syllables: first and third lines have five syllables and the second has seven:

> As we speak our lines,
> We hope they inspire your hearts.
> Springtime all year 'round.

Ask each member of your group to name the most meaningful response to such statements as "What America Means to Me, or Happiness Is—." For performance have each person repeat one of the series—sometimes rapidly, sometimes slowly—and always with enthusiasm: "Hot dogs . . . Cokes . . . the beach . . . Sonny . . . *and* Cher . . . Fridays . . ." An appealing idea is to have one person repeat the same thing every so often. For instance, "holding hands," each time with more stars in the eyes and more sweetness in the voice.

Encourage your people to write their own material. Use such formats as *The World of Carl Sandburg* by Norman Corwin and *Slightly Higher on the West Coast* by Frances Bardake and John Sinor. Work with the English classes and use the best from their writings—the interest in your Choric Theatre will increase by leaps and bounds because those students whose material you are using and their friends will not want to miss your next program.

REHEARSAL TECHNIQUES AND INTERPRETATION

It is, first of all, important that you approach your Choric Theatre group as prepared as possible in the material that you mean to use for the first rehearsal. Do not bog them down with lots of exercises that will become very useful and meaningful to them at a later rehearsal. The first rehearsal must be fun and exciting—they must know that Choric Theatre is work and only through work can they have successful programs—but the overall atmosphere must be one of joy. We think that the most important experience that happened to us was that of performing with the Macalester Drama Chorōs. They are so alive in every way—their interpretations and their movement. They are so electric in everything they do that our group came home with more initial drive than we could have inspired in a dozen rehearsals aimed at motivation. If you are demanding in achieving near-perfection in each of your selections, the audience will continue to instill desire in their applause and comments.

Probably the most important philosophy to get across to your group is that of perfection through repetition. It *is* difficult to maintain interest when material is repeated and repeated over and over again during rehearsal. However, if this repetition can result in some kind of recognizable improvement in a given rehearsal, your people, if they are earnest in their desire, will appreciate the work. We often let three or four drop out and go out in the "audience" during rehearsal to listen. They come back realizing that the group sounds "just great" and "so much better than when we are listening within the group."

To promote greater projection and enunciation, yell *"Spit,"* which is short and easy to say in a very minimal pause. The result is amazing: The words fairly fly out and across the auditorium—sharp, crisp, and meaningful. When the message is dragging and the tempo becomes more like tympani than like a snare drum, we suggest that they think about rinsing their mouths out with pure lemon juice, stretch the lips so that they tingle, and "taste the words on the end of your tongue." The result is generally 100 percent improvement. A good fast trot around the gym or stage or jumping calisthenics will revitalize everyone—material comes alive again.

One of our most intriguing techniques in performance is that of our attacks at the beginning of selections or after lengthy pauses. It is really a very simple trick. For each of our three voice quality sections we have one or two leaders. We call them personnel captains, and they have duties such as checking appearance for their section, handing out scripts, and keeping attendance records. Within the performance they direct the attacks. With a simple but sharp nod of the head they begin a selection. To keep their identity a secret and our technique a mystery, every member of the group sharply nods along with the leader. The result is strong attacks. It is also fun to have members of the audience ask how it is done. Very rarely is there a need for a director to stand between the chorōs and its audience. Unless the group numbers one hundred or more, the director has done his job in rehearsal and is *no longer needed during performance.* For the more serious material, a slower and less sharp nod is preferable.

The same kind of direction is used for bowing after material has been performed. The exception is that for bowing, the direction is from the waist instead of the neck and head. Use the numbers system: The first thrust backward is number one, the bend forward with the head down is number two and three, and the return to an upright position is number four. At the conclusion of a set of numbers, at the end of the program, or after an especially difficult number that we have directed, we will bow with the chorōs and then acknowledge the chorōs with a wave of the hand in their direction. Depending on the length and quality of the applause, we extend two or three fingers when we wave toward them. This means that the leaders will "take over" and have two or three successive bows after we have left the stage.

When material has reached near-perfection and you rehearse in a standing position, insist that your group stand in performance posture. They cannot expect to present a pleasing appearance at the last moment when they are before an audience. Two general rules: weight on both feet and scripts at a point just above the waist or at a point at the base of the rib cage. If scripts are not used, we have the boys stand with their hands behind them and then raised about two inches. The girls stand with their arms hanging comfortably at their sides. If you direct, do not begin until all eyes are on you, and insist that they remain on you until the selection is finished.

Rehearse with your facial muscles, too! Make all sorts of strange and fearsome faces! Get your group into the habit of automatic smiles, grimaces, and other facial responses within certain material. They cannot be expected to excite, please, warm, electrify, and become endeared to the audience if they interpret with their voices only and not with their whole selves!

Chapter VI

SAMPLE MATERIAL AND NOTES
FOR CHORIC THEATRE

We have included twelve representative poems in this chapter. Please be assured that there are a hundred and one ways of presenting each one of them. We have included notes to help you get started with them. Even with the notes you will sound different from other Choric Theatre groups and this is as it should be. Art is a personal thing and should be treated as such. There will be an overall style, hopefully, for your Choric Theatre—you will become known for particular pieces and your own particular ways of reading.

As with Readers' Theatre and Chamber Theatre material production rights, note that in the cases of most anthologies permission for reprinting must be obtained from the publisher. Always write to the publisher for permission to reprint and perform any kind of material for Choric Theatre. Many times the publisher will ask only that you give credit to the publisher in the printed program. Again, royalties are not usually preset for material other than regular play scripts.

We trust we have included enough material in Chapter V so that you may refer to it when questions arise concerning the material in this chapter. The important thing is that you enjoy the material you are reading and that you read with vitality and clearness.

You will find in the selections we have chosen that there are examples for reading in your group sections: light, medium, dark; solos; onomatopoetically; as one voice; children's selections; dialect; and surprise endings.* The possibilities are limitless and are subject to your imagination and talent.

---

* "A" means all voices; "L" light; "M" medium; and "D" dark.

Consider the Lily

In the evening, on Calvary, for love—	LM (Light and medium.)
On the hill our Saviour died—	
There came darkness from the heavens above.	(Make it dark.) (End high.)
Consider the lily.	A (Drop all voices.)
In the days before the act of love,	D "taught" high, "prayed" low.
Our Saviour taught and prayed;	
The spirit of God was to have descended as a dove.	(Enunciate carefully, whole line in one complete flow.)
Consider the lily.	A
In the sermon on the Mount—	A
Our Saviour was to declare	
"Take no thought for your life . . .	D
Behold the fowls of the air. . . ."	
Consider the lily.	A
On the eve of the greatest of sacrifices	A (Pause after "sacrifices.")
Our Saviour held communion	(No pause, go right on.)
With the twelve of His disciples.	
Consider the lily.	
Later—	A (Firm, long pause.)
"Away with Him!" they cried.	LM on quotation, A on "they cried." Quotations: loud, crowd-like.
"Crucify Him!"	
And Jesus bore the cross;	D
And on Golgotha they *did* crucify Him.	LM
Consider the lily.	A
And there were those who wept.	LM
And those who did cast lots;	D
Then—	A
"It is finished."	D
And He slept.	A
Consider the lily.	

Clayton E. Liggett

THE CRY

Oh, Brotherhood, Oh, Brotherhood,   A
In this we call Thy name;
It matters not the tint of face,   L
Nor creed of Godly fame.   A

Oh, Brotherhood, Oh, Brotherhood,   A
Be this the cry of man;
Be he yellow, black, or white   M: "Be he yellow," D: "black," L: "white"
Or reddened by Thy hand.   A

Oh, Brotherhood, In Brotherhood
We cry, but do not stand!
"I'm Catholic"—"I'm Jew"—"I'm Protes-
    tant."   Each quote: solo.
We're proud. But God! Thy hand!   A

Oh, Brotherhood, Oh, Brotherhood
Oh God, we call for Thee—
Call sons and daughters in Thy name
To strive for unity.

Oh, Brotherhood, Sweet Brotherhood,   D: "Oh,—"; L: "Sweet—"
We pledge our lives for thee;   A
We men of creeds—Oh, God, we work
That we may live with Thee.

Clayton E. Liggett
to Dr. Albert F. Hirsch, 1951

Out of the Night

We include this poem to illustrate the innumerable possibilities of onomatopoetic reading of words. Pay particular attention to the sounds of the italicized words. (Italicizing was not a part of the original printing of the poem; it is added here for you.)

Out of the *night,*
As a *bullet sharp,*
A train comes *tracing* through.
Winding down the endless tracks
It *thunders, cracks,* and *wails.*
Steadily *speeding,* ceaselessly *reeling*
Over the iron rails.

Out of the night,
As a *bullet sharp,*
A *whistle* wakens you.
Sharp and *cross* it *warns* its way
Through city, town, and vale,
Or *moans* in *mystic madness*
As *wind* in a *winter's gale.*

Clayton E. Liggett

Let your talents run rampant—overdo.

In most cases when you decide you are going to go through a work and really let yourselves go, you will find ways of reading that you will like and will keep for public performance.

TAKE MY HAND
By Doris C. Steffy

This is the first printing of Miss Steffy's "Take My Hand" other than in the *Colorado Education Review*. We include it because of its message as well as its literary merit. We have made use of 27 solo readers.

I'm born . . . Equal? Who wants equality?   Solo #1 A: "Equal" (solo continues.)
The others—no threat. I'm the baby. I smile.
I'm warm, fed, and dry. Equality? Keep it!   A: "Equality" (solo continues.)
This is my kingdom. I'm queen of my castle.
My castle—home.

I'm white and seven.   Solo #2
A traveling colored troupe arrives in town.
The adults look strange. There's a boy . . .
He's cute . . . He's just my size.
He's black as Dad's Sunday suit.
His eyes are big like a cow's.
He's got curly hair just huggin' his head!
I'm fascinated, I take his hand, we skip to-
    gether.
He can dance! I want to learn.
I love him—I take him home—they'll love
    him.
They don't. I'm sent to my room— He's sent
    packin'.
"Mustn't touch."   A

I'm a Sunday School girl.   A
The song goes
"Red and yellow, black and white,   Solo #3 (sing)
They are precious in His sight."
Who's they? The newspaper?   A
The sport section's yellow. It's read.
It's black and white—good joke.
Must tell my friends.

I'm a Methodist.   A
A Southern colored college wants an open
    date.
They'll come and sing.
Just one small item—We're to put them up
    overnight.
Who'll volunteer?—the silence deafens.   Solo: "Who'll volunteer?", pause, A
One smug parishioner will house two girls.   Solo #5
Who wants the boys? We can't take 'em.   Solo #6, Solo #7
Our Daddy's dead . . . who'd protect us?   Solo #7
Besides no niggers would sleep in a funeral   A
    home—
They're superstitious.   L
Sorry, no open date; enclosed find check.   A

164

I'm skilled in basketball.   Solo #8
We're cooperative. We're winning games.
That girl playing guard on the other team—
     she's colored.
Does she smell different?
She falls . . . her ankle's twisted.
I turn away—the others will help.
I'm little—they're stronger,
She needs to be carried. Let them!
Mustn't touch . . . she's different.   A

I'm in college.   LM
The war is on. It's exciting.
We're fighting! For what?
The air corps arrives. They're young. So am
     I.
It's gay, delightful.
I'm awakened by marching feet.
It's snowing. They sing:
          Hep-2-3-4 Hep-2-3-4   D (D continue with "Hep-2-3-4" through
Cadence count 3-4   D "threatened"—pause.)
I'm warm. I'm alive!
Some will die—I don't know them.
I'm not threatened. I'm a girl.   LM "I'm a girl."

School subjects, routine.   Solo (girl): #9, #10
Dates, movies, Cokes, this is life!   #11, #12, #13, #14
One squadron moves out; another moves   LM
     in—
Excitement! Youth! Men!   #15, #16, #17

My brother joins—we're represented.   A
He's stationed stateside.
A letter . . . the boy next door—
Killed in action. What action?   L: "What action?"
Where are we fighting? What for?   A L: "What for?"
He never was quick—probably got confused.   A
I'm alive—live for today.
I can get tires, gas, and meat stamps.
It's WHO you know. Does WHAT matter?   L: "It's WHO you know." A: "Does WHAT
                                                          matter?"

D-Day J-Day Happy day.
The war is over. We won.
The boys come back . . . they're older.
Too settled. Too serious. I like the uniform.
War bonds, saving stamps—for what?
I miss the thrills, despise routine. The flag is
     folded.
The war is over.

The headlines scream—"Rosenbergs!"   LM A: "Rosenbergs!"
Sounds Jewish—just little people.   LM

What did they do? Sold out? To whom? On America?

Solos: #18, #19, #20
#21

The flag is folded. Worth of the individual?

LM

Traitors! Spys! Fry 'em!

A

I'm a teacher.

A

I'm in control. I like discipline.

I choose helpers, the biggest boys.

A dirty boy . . . he spits on kids . . .

Note to parents "Hasn't adjusted to the group.

Solo: quotation #22

Recommendation—try another school."

I've won again.

A

I'm clever.

A

Summer school is different . . .

A few Negroes enroll.

We're on the playground. Join hands for a circle.

The circle is broken—the black boy stands alone.

To take his hand? Mustn't touch.

We change the game, running games to meet the need.

Whose need? My need, to save face.

I'm successful, a brilliant teacher.

We're having fun.

I'm on sabbatical.

I pay tuition and plan my program.

Sociology—sounds big—I'll take it.

Tenets of democracy . . . I must know five:

Worth of the individual, equality for all, co-operation, reason.

Solos: #23, #24, #25
#26

(Oh sure. Heard 'em all my life.)

A

Best of all—hope for the future.

Solo #27

Must keep them straight.

A

What do they mean? Who cares? I passed!

Of what worth knowledge!

Hey, Fascists!

DM

Wait for me! I'm duck soup. I'll join your forces.

I'm educated, I'm white, I'm American, I'm better!

LM

Take my hand, I'll wave your flag.

A

Permission granted for reprint by Doris C. Steffy and *Colorado Education Review*.

THE LORD'S PRAYER

From A Man Dies *by E. C. Marvin M.A.*

Our Father,
Our Father in Heaven,
Hallowed be Your Name.

Your kingdom come,
Your will be done,
In earth as it is in Heaven.

Our Father,
Give us this day,
Give us our daily bread,

And forgive us the harm
That we do to others,
When we forgive those that harm us.

Don't test us past our breaking point,
But keep us from the grip of wrong.

For in Your Hand
Is the Power and the Glory
For ever and ever, Amen.

Our Father,
Our Father in Heaven,
Hallowed be Your Name.
For Yours is the Kingdom,
The Power and the Glory
For ever and ever, Amen.

Permission granted for reprint by
E. C. Marvin.

This is a *must* in our repertoire. We use it as an opening when we appear for area church groups. The adaptation is vital to young people.

Use all punctuation as a pause marking.

Very rapid.

Prayerfully, pause.

Start to build.
Strong
Stronger, strongest—go right through to the "Amen" without a pause. "Amen" should be said with finality. Then pause and a very soft "Amen."

O LITTLE MAN

O little man, with funny eyes,
    And mouth as wide as long,
What makes you look so sad today?
    Oh, I see, you've no nose!
        What's wrong?

O little man, with funny eyes,
    And mouth—O, but wait!
What's happened to your eyes, I fear
    You must have met your fate!

O little man, you've gone your way
    But I'll remember you—
Remember you were here one day
    Little cloud, then vanished
        far from view.

Clayton E. Liggett

All voices throughout.

Read as though to a group of very small children—a children's hour at the library—wide-eyed and with amazement.

ONE HEART

Use the onomatopoeia of *Out of the Night* and the pauses you have learned in reading the other poems.

Make the pauses abnormally long.

Make the attacks of the initial words in each phrase or sentence true and clear.

Make one reading different from the next.

Watch your director.

Recall "Rehearsal techniques" in Chapter V and use them.

The feeling of the room was heavy. The soft flickering light in the obsolete corner seemed to fill every part of the room with a sympathetic, longing comfort. The solitude gave way to only a soft continuous weeping. It got no louder—no softer—only a steady whimpering—as a puppy, knowing not why his master had struck him.

In the center of the room stood a konopeion;[1] on it lay the slim figure of a girl—a very young girl—yet very old as she experienced omega.

A broken heart sat in vigil, a heart so full of grief and love it dared not stay as a whole. The weeping continued—still not hysterical, but continuously—continuously weeping—weeping long into the night.

Quietly, without announcement, the light flickered and died—the room lay quiet—utterly quiet.

Clayton E. Liggett

---

[1] Canopy bed.

169

This Night of Ours

The twilight ascends,
The snow drifts slowly down;
Beneath the moonlit sky, my way I wend
While hush and still abound.

A

Read straight through to "hush" then pause,
"and still" pause.

I'm not alone in this night of ours,
There are others this night who rejoice
In singing their carols for the pleasure of
   others,
Verbally their joy is voiced.

Read through to the end of the verse without
pauses.

Within they burst with pride.
Every eye sparkles, harboring lores;
Every mouth sings wishes wide,
For glorious is this night of ours.

Attention to "sparkles" and "lores."

Accent "is."

Our Saviour's birth—His love—His might—
Are everywhere this holy night.

Pause at each dash.

Clayton E. Liggett

By the Heavens Above

The moon shines bright from the heavens
    above,
The stars sparkle clear and near;
And I ponder the scene long ago, far away
Of the new-born Lord in the manger He
    lay.

The moon? Same moon. And the stars? The
    same.   *Exaggerate the questions.*
Warmed softly the Bethlehem scene.   *Make the answers final.*
And it thrills me to think I may always view
The holiness of the heavens our Saviour
    knew.

Holy? Yes, holy I say,
For you see of all that could tell   *Continue through to "love."*
Of the nativity scene we know and love
Uncountable stories are held by the heavens   *Pause after "held."*
    above.

                Clayton E. Liggett

CHRISTMAS IS A THOUSAND THINGS

The notes are not complete. We have marked only places that we feel particularly important.

Christmas is a thousand things:	A
It's a winter's night,	MD
And an angel song,	L
A giant star,	D
And tiny stable, a manger and straw—	L
And swaddling clothes.	A (hard attack on "and.")

Christmas is a chime,	M
A boy soprano,	L
And *Silent Night*.	MD
Carolers . . . and the first Noël.	A
The tinkle of a bell on a sleigh . . .	L
Of a coin in a cup.	M

Christmas is Dickens	MD
And Scrooge	D
And Tiny Tim.	L
It's holly on the door,	M
A candle in the window,	D
The scent of pine,	L
And the sparkle of tinsel.	A

Christmas is red	M Fast, carry over from line
And green	D to line through "silver."
And blue	M
And silver.	L
Christmas is white.	A
Christmas is cards	M
And ribbon and tissue paper.	L Make it wind like ribbon.
It's a trip home, an open latch, a handclasp.	A Long pauses at commas.

It's giblets	A
And biscuits,	L
Cranberries	A
And mincemeat pie.	SOLO
Christmas is cold and warmth, forgiveness, and a smile.	A

Christmas is a prayer—	L
A renewed plea for ancient hope.	M
For peace on earth . . . and good-will toward men.	A Long pause after "earth."

Anonymous

172

STOPPING BY WOODS ON A SNOWY EVENING

This poem is included because we never do a program of Choric Theatre without using it. It is not what we would call our "theme" number, but it is a favorite, and we are becoming known for it. The decision to use it in each program was not made arbitrarily; it was an accidental unanimous decision: in looking through our previous programs we found that *Stopping by Woods* was always included.

Whose woods these are I think I know.　(Pause after "are.")
His house is in the village though;
He will not see me stopping here　(No pause.)
To watch his woods fill up with snow.

My little horse must think it queer　(Quicken the first two lines, no pauses.)
To stop without a farmhouse near
Between the woods and frozen lake
The darkest evening of the year.

He gives his harness bells a shake　(Quicken first two lines.)
To ask if there is some mistake.
The only other sound's the sweep
Of easy wind and downy flake.　(Watch special words.)

The woods are lovely, dark and deep.　(Pay particular attention to "lovely," "dark,"
But I have promises to keep,　and "deep.")
And miles to go before I sleep,　Pause.
And miles to go before I sleep.　Pause after "go."

Robert Frost

LUCY LAKE

Lawsamassy, for heaven's sake!
Have you never heard of Lucy Lake?
Lucy is fluffy and fair and cozy,
Lucy is like a budding posy.
Lucy speaks with a tiny lisp,
Lucy's mind is a will-o'-the-wisp.
Lucy is just as meek as a mouse,
Lucy lives in a darling house,
With a darling garden and darling fence,
And a darling faith in the future tense.
A load of hay, or a crescent moon,
And she knows that things will be better
    soon.
Lucy resigns herself to sorrow
In building character for tomorrow.

Lucy tells us to carry on,
It's always darkest before the dawn.
A visit to Lucy's bucks you up,
Helps you swallow the bitterest cup.
Lucy Lake is meek as a mouse.
Let's go over to Lucy's house,
And let's lynch Lucy!

Ogden Nash

From *Verses from 1929 On* by Ogden Nash. By permission of Little, Brown and Co., copyright 1938 by Ogden Nash. Originally appeared in *The New Yorker*.

Quite by accident the Drama Chorōs developed a southern accent with *Lucy Lake*. We use this poem for girls only. We have the boys sit down on the risers during this reading. They "pop" up later.

Very rapid through "tense."

So slow!

Very final.

L
M
L
LM
L
LM As though the poem had ended.
A   Boys stand and everyone says last line gnashed, loud and clear, through the teeth!

THE SHAGGY STORIES

As the *Shaggy Story* is announced, the entire Chorōs goes into a "B" formation sitting on the floor around the reader.

The Shaggy Tern Story

On the seashore of a remote island in the Pacific there lived a colony of terns. They were a happy, contented flock, minded their own business and in their own words they thought

Storyteller

(Our storyteller told *The Shaggy Tern Story* in Bronx dialect!)

"Happiness is for the birds."

Chorōs   (No dialect.)

This happy, contented flock spent carefree hours soaring in the skies, catching fishes and turning their eggs every two or three hours because

It was one of Mother Nature's laws.

However, things change as they so often do . . . a family moved onto their little isle and built themselves a cottage beside the deep blue water.

(wah-dah)

They had a son and a daughter.

(dah-dah)

The daughter was nice but the little boy was a pest. He loved to throw stones at the birds, which was upsetting, but perhaps his little misdemeanors can be condoned, because he'd heard the old adage

"Never leave a tern unstoned."

(Say the line and within the rhythm of the line finish it off with a sick smile—smirk!)

Shaggy Indian Story

In a remote spot in the forest primeval, an Indian brave named Shortcake supported his family by hunting the wild deer and catching fishes.

He was sweet, amiable and never vicious.

Because he was never vicious, he earned the affection and respect of his fellow tribesmen and was often invited to sit in the tribal council and smoke the peace pipe.

He was the civic-minded type.

One day the news was flashed via smoke signals and tom-toms that he had wrestled with a grizzly and when the grizzly had him downed,

He went to the happy hunting ground.

The chiefs of the five nations gathered to help with the ceremony, but his squaw refused and smiling through a tear as tho' her heart would break, said,

"No, squaw bury Shortcake."

Permission for reprint granted by The Miles Kimball Company of Oshkosh, Wisconsin.

(We finish as in *Tern* but with a "sick" *"huh."*)

Sample Program Material

This list constitutes our repertoire for one season.

The House I Live In, Lewis Allan
These I Have Loved from *The Great Lover,* Rupert Brooke
How Jack Found That Beans May Go Back on a Chap, Carryl
Anyone Lived in a Pretty How Town, e.e. cummings
The Listeners, Walter de la Mare
The Road Not Taken, Robert Frost
Stopping by Woods on a Snowy Evening, Robert Frost
The Dream Song from *Iolanthe,* W. S. Gilbert
The Lord's Prayer from *A Man Dies,* Hooper and Marvin
The Ghost of the Buffaloes, Vachel Lindsay
Ballad of the Happy Christmas Wind, Mary Madeleva
The King's Breakfast, A. A. Milne
Tale of Custard the Dragon, Ogden Nash
Lucy Lake, Ogden Nash
The People Upstairs, Ogden Nash
Whales, Ogden Nash
Pediatric Reflections, Ogden Nash
The Maid Servant at the Inn, Dorothy Parker
Sounds to Remember, E. K. Povenmire
Respectable People, Carl Sandburg
The Hongdorshes, Carl Sandburg
If You Hate a Man, Carl Sandburg
Fables, Parables, and High Nonsense, Carl Sandburg
To Be or Not to Be from *Hamlet,* Shakespeare
In the Carpenter's Shop, Sara Teasdale
O Captain! My Captain!, Walt Whitman
The Shaggy Stories, with special permission from The Miles Kimball Co.
Santa Claus and the Mouse, Anon.
Christmas Is a Thousand Things, Anon.
The Friendly Beasts, Anon.
'Twas the Night Before Christmas, Adapted
The Lion Hunt, Anon.

Program material may be selected on the basis of subject, season, holiday, theme, such as the worth of man, or for just plain fun. The material is worth reading if it catches your imagination, means something special, or emotionally moves you.

Chapter VII

IN SUMMARY

Probably the most important point to remember in any form of Concert Theatre is that you want to go into it with your heart—be creative first of all and academic later. Nothing can stop you if you really have the desire to give a great deal of enjoyment and take a great deal too!

Here is just one result from high-school work in Concert Theatre. The writer of the following report is Miss Marla Painter of Del Mar, California, a student at San Diego State College. Miss Painter was a member of the San Dieguito Drama Chorōs.

The function of Wildwood Nature Camp in Barre, Massachusetts, is to promote a child's wonder in his environment; particularly, in the natural world. As a counselor at Wildwood, I was responsible for a didactic program presented at the end of each two-week session. It was to be an introspection, by a small group of campers for the entire camp, of their intellectual and spiritual growth within the realm of nature. This, of course, included their lives with other people, God, the woods they were camping in, and their overall consciousness. Although this is a difficult project to present to a child, the results were beautifully astounding.

I chose Drama Chorōs as the medium through which the children could creatively communicate their dialogue with their environment. In this way, they could address not only their audience, but themselves, others in the chorōs, and even the

fauna and flora of the woods. In choosing the material for the script, the campers and I found our most adventurous task. Having in mind the meaning of Vespers—a group expression of camper's individual feelings—I decided that they should choose or compose their own material. Hence, I gathered together a variety of books, from *The Little Prince* by Antoine de Saint Exupéry, to poetry of Yevgeny Yevtushenko, to the nature poetry of Gwen Frostic. During our meetings the campers and I read, picked and practiced musical selections, and those who wished to, wrote. When a selection was found by anyone, its merits were discussed by the group and, if all agreed, we assimilated it into the program. We also decided on any alterations, i.e., if another person would deliver the cutting or how it would be cut. Emphasis was placed upon one's dialogue with his natural environment; however, the children also desired to express feelings dealing with other human beings, morality and, appropriately, nature conservation. When the material was chosen, I organized the program and blocked it. Rehearsals then began and changes were entered into the script. The program was presented in a cleared area of the woods, which was fashioned into a "chapel" with crude benches facing a mound of mossy rocks and tree stumps. This served as a most effective stage. The chorōs delivered the material in a varied, energetic manner. They changed stage positions with con-

Plate XVIII. *Choric Theatre Group, Wildwood Nature Camp, Barre, Massachusetts.*

trasts in heights and groupings to effectively partner the oral variation. A short Haiku, for instance, was delivered by one person standing alone while others sat upon the rocks that served as their stage. Upon the Haiku's finish, a group of perhaps six, or even all fifteen, members, would arise in groupings of three to recite a hearty chanting sound by Walt Whitman. A verbally inconspicuous narrator was often effective to give gentle introductions and to coordinate the often fragmentary pieces of literature. He was never the center of attention and what he said was desirably in the background. Sporadically, one member or a small group of the chorōs would walk down from the main group to recite. The emphasis was on a variety of movement to complement the variety of oral activity.

On the afternoon of the performance, the program usually began after the audience had become completely silent (all were asked to become silent upon entering the "chapel" area.) The members of the chorōs used individual trees as their "backstage." With one person beginning as a signal to the rest, the chorōs entered from behind trees in each direction and took their spot upon the rocky stage. The program then began, quickly paced, with emphasis placed on comparison of imagery and contrast of ideas. It was broken up by musical selections, which varied from Baroque flute solos to folk songs on a recorder, to guitar trios and even some jazz trumpet. In discussing the effect that we wanted, we decided that a collage of thought and sensory stimulus was the goal. I stressed to the campers the importance of maintaining an energetic pace while grasping each word and presenting their gift to the audience with personal care—an ambitious goal for children who generally had no dramatic experience. Although the experiment was far from perfect, each attempt grew better with new techniques being revealed each time. More importantly, the campers in the chorōs grew immeasurably by the experience—sometimes in ways that transcended the craft that they were learning. Moreover, with the group song or hymn and the silent meditation that followed the performance, I was certain that the audience had received some form of stimulus for feeling, thinking, and growing as human creatures.

The possibilities for use of all areas of Concert Theatre are limitless: church groups, playground, summer recreation programs, church camps, elementary school.

We might take the opportunity right here to mention Choreographic Worship, which many churches are incorporating into their young peoples' groups. The techniques of this kind of dance are deliberate and not impossible for anyone who has not had the benefit of formal dance training. To couple the Choreographic Worship with Choric Theatre is an exciting and dynamic form of interpretation. We have taken techniques from this dance form and used them in the Choric Theatre—therefore Drama Chorōs. To our knowledge no formal text has been written on the techniques of Choreographic Worship; however, a little investigation and questioning will uncover a group somewhere who can help you.

Now that you have tasted the various aspects of Concert Theatre and have found the vast possibilities of the three areas, we hope that you are still excited and "ready to continue." Now you know what kinds of fun you are going to have, the enjoyment you can give (the sweet smell of success), and the talent you can develop for yourselves and your fellow students—theatre students to be sure.

Remember: "Do!"

MATERIAL FOR CHORIC THEATRE *

EARLY AMERICAN UNIT

Christopher Columbus, by Rosemary and Stephen Vincent Benét
A light poem, pointed at how Columbus expected to find China.

Landing of the Pilgrim Fathers, by Felicia Dorothea Hermans
A poem directed toward expressing what the Pilgrims sought in the New World.

Concord Hymn, by Ralph Waldo Emerson
A poem dedicated to those who died for freedom at Concord.

The Green Mountain Boys, by William Cullen Bryant
A spirit of rebellion as shown by Ethan Allen and his Green Mountain Boys.

The Yankee's Return from Camp, by Edward Bangs
The poem that became the song *Yankee Doodle.*

The Fourth of July, by John Pierpont
An expression of the rejoicing at the adoption of the Declaration of Independence.

The Battle of Trenton, Anon.
A poem telling of the battle of Trenton, and how it gave heart to the patriots.

Defeat and Victory, by Wallace Rice
Captain James Lawrence's famous saying "Don't give up the ship" is used to express the spirit of Americans at war.

Old Ironsides, by Oliver Wendell Holmes
Written as a protest to the plan for destroying the ship *Constitution.* Tells of the ship's past glories.

O Beautiful, My Country, by Frederick L. Hosmer
The expression of a man who sees in his country the beauty of its freedom.

WESTWARD GROWTH UNIT

Daniel Boone, by Arthur Guiterman
The life of Daniel Boone, containing many facts and expressing the spirit of the westward movement.

Lewis and Clark, by Rosemary Benét
The adventures of the Lewis and Clark expedition.

Pioneers, O Pioneers, by Walt Whitman
A poem that captures the spirit and courage of the early settlers.

The Gold-Seekers, by Hamlin Garland
A poem telling of the rush to California for gold, and the hardships and despair that had to be faced.

Bill Peters, Anon.
A cowboy ballad depicting the adventure of driving a stage in the West.

The Defense of the Alamo, by Joaquin Miller
A poem that combines the spirit of the Alamo with the names of the famous men who fought there.

The Passing Herd, by Kenneth C. Kaufman
This poem expresses the feelings of a young boy as he experiences the great cattle drives of the West.

Song of the Forerunner, by Karle Widso Baker
A poem depicting the type of people who settled Texas, and the dream they had of what their state would be.

---

* Listed in chronological order.

Betsy from Pike, Anon.

A ballad that describes the trip from Pike County, Missouri, to California.

Thunderdrums, Anon.

This poem is the chant that the Chippewa Indians used in their war dances. It reflects the spirit of the Indian resistance to the white man's advance on their lands.

CIVIL WAR UNIT

John Brown's Body, by Charles Sprague Hall
This poem was set to music and used as a marching song during the war. It symbolizes the North's feeling toward slavery.

We Conquer or Die, by James Pierpont
A call to arms for all southerners to defend their freedom.

The Brigade Must Not Know, Sir, Anon.
This poem tells of the fear that the news of Stonewall Jackson's death might get to the troops. It is a dedication to his courage and inspiration.

Gettysburg Address, by Abraham Lincoln
Although this is not a poem in the strictest sense, it can be done well in Choric Theatre.

Sherman's in Savannah, by Oliver Wendell Holmes
A poem expressing joy at the success of the Northern Armies.

Clara Barton, by Rosemary and Vincent Benét
A poem depicting the accomplishments of Clara Barton, and her spirit to humanity.

The Surrender at Appomattox, by Herman Melville
The meaning of victory and peace are expressed in this poem.

O Captain! My Captain!, by Walt Whitman
An expression of grief at the loss of President Lincoln.

The Conquered Banner, by Abram Joseph Ryan
This poem expresses the sorrow and weariness of the South at the end of the war.

The Blue and the Gray, by Francis Miles Finch
This poem reflects the idea that respect should be given all those who fought in the Civil War.

AMERICA AS A WORLD POWER UNIT

How Cyrus Laid the Cable, by John Godfrey Saxe
The story of the struggle to lay the Atlantic cable.

My People Came to This Country, by Burt Struthers
The expression of the feelings of a man for the peace and safety America gave him.

The Name of Old Glory, by James Whitcomb Riley
A poem telling how our flag came to be known as Old Glory.

The Thinker, by Berton Braley
An expression of the importance of man even in an industrial era.

Abraham Lincoln Walks at Midnight, by Vachel Lindsay
A poem directed toward the idea that America, as symbolized by Lincoln, should be concerned with the happenings in Europe.

Armistice Day, by Roselle M. Montgomery
A sober thought about the price we paid for the Armistice.

The New Crusade, by Catharine Lee Bates
This poem presents the idea that World War I would be the war to end all wars.

What Does It Mean to Be an American?, by Roselle M. Montgomery
A poem telling of the great inheritances we as Americans should live up to.

The United States in 2033, by Rosemary and Stephen Benét
A look ahead that gives us a viewpoint of history and our place in it.

Prayer of a Soldier in France, by Joyce Kilmer
This poem expresses the thoughts of a soldier as he compares his suffering and sacrifices to those that Christ suffered for him.

** Albright, H. Darkes. *Working up a Part.* New York: Houghton Mifflin, 1959.

Anderson, Virgil A. *Training the Speaking Voice.* New York: Oxford, 1961.

* Arnott, Peter D. *Introduction to Greek Theatre.* Bloomington, Indiana: Indiana University Press, 1959.

Bacon, Wallace A. *The Art of Interpretation.* New York: Holt, Rinehart and Winston, 1966.

** Bavely, Ernest, ed. *Dramatic Director's Handbook.* Rev. ed., The National Thespian Society, Cincinnati, 1949.

** Boleslavsky, Richard. *Acting: The First Six Lessons.* New York: Theatre Arts, 1933.

** Boyle, Walden P. *Central and Flexible Staging.* Berkeley, California: University of California Press, 1956.

* Brockett, Oscar G. *The Theatre: An Introduction.* New York: Holt, Rinehart and Winston, 1964.

Brooks, Keith, Eugene Bahn, and L. La-Mont Okey. *The Communicative Act of Oral Interpretation.* Boston: Allyn and Bacon, Inc., 1967.

** Browne, E. Martin. *Religious Drama 2.* New York: Meridian, 1958.

** Cartmell, Van H. *Amateur Theatre: A Guide for Actor and Director.* Van Nostrand, 1961.

** Cerf, Bennett, ed. *Thirty Famous One-act Plays.* New York: Modern Library, 1943.

** ———. *Twenty-four Favorite One-Act Plays.* Barnes and Noble, New York, 1958.

Chekhov, Michael. *To the Actor.* New York: Harper and Bros., 1953.

Cheney, Sheldon. *The Theatre: Three Thousand Years of Drama, Acting, and Stagecraft.* New York: David MacKay, 1952.

** Chute, Marchette. *Shakespeare of London.* New York: E. P. Dutton, 1949.

Cole, Toby and Helen Krich Chinoy. *Directors on Directing.* Indianapolis, Indiana: Bobbs-Merrill, 1963.

———. *Actors on Acting.* New York: Crown, 1949.

* Cole, Toby, ed. *Acting: A Handbook of the Stanislavski Method.* New York, Crown, 1955.

Cosgrove, Frances, ed. *Scenes for Student Actors.* New York: Samuel French, 1936–42, 6 vols.

Davis, Jed H. and Mary Jane Watkins. *Children's Theatre: Play Production for the Child Audience.* New York: Harper, 1960.

Dean, Alexander. *The Fundamentals of Play Directing.* New York: Holt, Rinehart and Winston, 1965.

* Dietrich, John E. *Play Direction.* Englewood Cliffs, New Jersey: Prentice-Hall, 1953.

Eisman, P. "High School Dramatics Program," *High Points.* 40:50–53, May, 1958.

Gassner and Sweetkind. *Introducing the Drama.* New York: Holt, Rinehart and Winston.

———. *Tragedy, History, and Romance.* New York: Holt, Rinehart and Winston.

* Gassner, John. *Producing the Play.* Rev. ed., New York: Holt, Rinehart and Winston, 1953.

* ———. *Masters of the Drama.* New York: Dover, 1954.

Gielgud, John. *Stage Directions.* New York: Random House, 1963.

** Gillette, A. S. *Stage Scenery.* New York: Harper, 1950.

** Gorchakov, Nikolai M. and Miriam Goldina (trans.). *Stanislavski Directs.* New York: Funk and Wagnalls, 1954.

** Gruver, Bert. *The Stagemanager's Hand-*

---

* Begin your theatre library with these books.
** These should be purchased next.

book. New York: Drama Book Shop, 1953.

** Gullan, Marjorie. *Choral Speaking*. London: Methuen and Co. Ltd., 1961.

** Guthrie, Tyrone. *A Life in the Theatre*. New York: McGraw-Hill, 1959.

* ———. *Lecture on Directing a Play*. New York: Folkways Records and Service Corporation, 1962.

Hake, Herbert V. *Here's How*. Evanston, Illinois: Row Peterson, 1958.

** Hamilton, Edith. *Mythology*. New York: Mentor Books, 1952.

* Hewitt, Barnard. *Theatre U.S.A.* New York: McGraw-Hill, 1959.

Hughes, Glenn. *The Penthouse Theatre: Its History and Technique*. Seattle: University of Washington, 1958.

** Jones, Robert Edmond. *The Dramatic Imagination*. New York: Theatre Arts, 1941.

* Kozelka, Paul. *The Theatre Student: Directing*. New York: Richards Rosen Press, 1968.

Kozelka, Paul, ed. *Fifteen American One Acts*. New York: Washington Square Press, 1961.

** Latham, Jean Lee. *Do's and Don't's of Drama: 555 Pointers for Beginning Actors and Directors*. Chicago: Dramatic Publishing Co., 1935.

Lease, Ruth and Geraldine B. Siks. *Creative Dramatics in Home, School, and Community*. New York: Harper.

* Lee, Charlotte I. *Oral Interpretation*. Boston: Houghton, Mifflin, 1959.

Little and Gassner. *Reading and Staging the Play*. New York: Holt, Rinehart and Winston.

** McGaw, Charles J. *Acting Is Believing*. New York: Holt, Rinehart and Winston, 1955.

* Moon, Samuel, ed. *One Acts: Short Plays of the Modern Theatre*. New York: Grove Press.

** Moore, Sonia. *The Stanislavski Method*. New York: Viking Press, 1960.

* Nagler, A. M. *A Source Book in Theatrical History*. New York: Dover, 1952.

** Ommanney, Katharine. *The Stage and the School*. 4th ed. New York: McGraw-Hill, 1963.

Pendleton, Ralph, ed., *The Theatre of Robert Edmond Jones*. Middleton, Connecticut: Wesleyan University Press, 1958.

Selden, Samuel. *First Steps in Acting*. New York: Appleton-Century-Crofts, 1947.

———. *Shakespeare: A Player's Handbook of Short Scenes*. New York: Holiday House, 1960.

Seyler, Athene and Stephen Haggard. *The Craft of Comedy*. New York: Theatre Arts, 1946.

** Shank, Theodore J., ed. *A Digest of 500 Plays: Plot Outlines and Production Notes*. New York: Crowell-Collier. 1963.

Sherman, Allan. *A Gift of Laughter*. New York: Atheneum, 1965.

** Siks, Geraldine Brain. *Creative Dramatics*. New York: Harper and Row, 1958.

Siks, Geraldine B. and Hazel B. Dunnington. *Children's Theatre and Creative Dramatics*. Seattle: University of Washington Press, 1961.

———. *Creative Dramatics, an Art for Children*. New York: Harper, 1958.

Simley, Anne. *Folk Tales to Tell or Read Aloud*. Minneapolis, Minnesota: Burgess Publishing Co., 1963.

* ———. *Oral Interpretation Handbook*. Minneapolis, Minnesota: Burgess Publishing Co., 1960.

** *Simon's Directory of Theatrical Materials, Services and Information*. New York: Package Publicity Service, 1963.

Southern, Richard. *The Open Stage*. New York: Theatre Arts, 1959.

* Spolin, Viola. *Improvisation for the Theatre: Handbook of Teaching and Directing Techniques*. Evanston, Illinois: Northwestern University Press, 1963.

** Stanislavski, Constantin. *An Actor Prepares*. New York: Theatre Arts, 1946.

** ———. *Building a Character*. New York: Theatre Arts, 1949.

** ———. *Creating a Role*. New York: Theatre Arts, 1961.

** Strickland, F. Cowles. *The Technique of Acting*. New York: McGraw-Hill, 1956.

** Teeter, Robert, et al. *Course of Study in Theatre Arts at the Secondary School Level*. Washington, D.C.: American Educational Theatre Association, 1963.

** Ward, Winifred. *Theatre for Children*. Anchorage, Kentucky: Children's Theatre Press, 1958.

** ———. *Playmaking with Children from Kindergarten through Junior High School*. 2d ed. New York: Appleton-Century-Crofts, 1957.

* Webster, Margaret. *Shakespeare without Tears*. Boston: Fawcett, 1942.

Whiting, Frank M. *An Introduction to the Theatre*. New York: Harper and Row, 1954.

Woods, M. S. "Creative Dramatics," *National Education Association Journal.* 48:52–53, May, 1959.

Zachar, Irwin J. *Plays as Experience: One-act Plays for the Secondary School.* New York: Odyssey Press, 1962.